You were made to encounter the God of miracles. In her new book, Tammy Hotsenpiller will lead you into a place of deeper trust, obedience, and faith as you learn to seek God through a season of fasting. *Fasting for Miracles* will stir your faith for the miraculous and take you closer to the only One who can do the impossible. I recommend this book to every believer who wants to encounter more of God!

—Dr. Ché Ahn
Senior Pastor, Harvest Rock Church, Pasadena, California; President, Harvest International Ministry; International Chancellor, Wagner University

The Holy Spirit is palpable in the pages of *Fasting for Miracles.* Tammy Hotsenpiller guides the reader on a spiritual exploration of their faith, commitment, and devotion to God as they fast for twenty-one days, seeking His voice and divine intervention through Scripture and prayer. She also brings to light the incredible truth that the enemy tries so hard to suppress, which is that miracles are not just for biblical times, but for *today.*

Her message is to seek God in our purest form and call for nationwide prayer and fasting—an anointed message and Spirit-filled act of faith, affirming our belief that God does and will perform miracles for those who are obedient to His will and *believe.*

—Dave Scarlett
Chairman and Founder, His Glory Ministries

Almost everyone I talk to needs a miracle right now, but so many people will possibly wait in a type of hope in the same way that lottery ticket purchasers wait for their ticket numbers to be called—it's not an activated, faith-filled process so it won't give them the result they are desperate for. Those who get miracles that are consistent are some of the most deliberate people I know, and this book by Tammy will put you

on track to love a lifestyle of miracles if you will embrace the sacrificial life of fasting. She lays it out beautifully and makes it simple, and I was reignited while going through it for my own lifestyle of fasting. I highly recommend this for families, group study, and everyone who wants more access to the divine nature of Christ.

—SHAWN BOLZ
TV HOST; AUTHOR; PODCASTER; PROPHETIC VOICE

I have had the honor of receiving this phenomenal book, and I have to say, what an insightful and provoking read it is! In *Fasting for Miracles*, Tammy Hotsenpiller leads you on a step-by-step guide of how to skillfully open the door to the miracles of God in your life. You'll be strengthened in your belief that all things are truly possible and equipped with the insight on how to get God's attention.

—JONATHAN ISAAC
NBA FORWARD, ORLANDO MAGIC; AUTHOR, *WHY I STAND*

Fasting is not simply a strike from eating food. It is a demand placed upon heaven for breakthrough, healing, deliverance, signs, and wonders. In this book, Tammy will challenge and encourage you to incorporate the lost art of fasting into the rhythm of your life. Expect a miracle!

—SEAN FEUCHT
FOUNDER, LET US WORSHIP

My friend Tammy Hotsenpiller is a prayer warrior! She is the person you call when you want someone to pray for you, and you know without a doubt she will. She has lived the message of her new book, *Fasting for Miracles*, for many years. Her experience and wisdom and the depth of her prayer life are evident in this book. This message will increase your prayer life and your hunger to see God move in miraculous ways!

—KIM WALKER-SMITH
WORSHIP ARTIST

I am honored to endorse my friend Tammy Hotsenpiller's new book, *Fasting for Miracles*. There are few in my life who understand the importance and significance of fasting like Tammy does. She has taught on and studied this subject matter for years, and there is tremendous fruit as a result. Tammy truly walks this out in her own life and ministry. This book will cause you to grow and go deeper in your walk, as well as equip you to be set up for success as a believer in this critical hour. I highly encourage you to read this book.

—TODD COCONATO
FOUNDER, TODD COCONATO MINISTRIES;
HOST, *THE TODD COCONATO SHOW*

FASTING
—— FOR ——
MIRACLES

TAMMY
HOTSENPILLER

CHARISMA
HOUSE

Most Charisma Media products are available at special quantity discounts for bulk purchase for sales promotions, premiums, fund-raising, and educational needs. For details, call us at (407) 333-0600 or visit our website at www.charismamedia.com.

FASTING FOR MIRACLES by Tammy Hotsenpiller
Published by Charisma House, an imprint of Charisma Media
600 Rinehart Road, Lake Mary, Florida 32746

Visit the author's website at tammyhotsenpiller.com.

Cataloging-in-Publication Data is on file with the Library of Congress.
International Standard Book Number: 978-1-63641-174-3
E-book ISBN: 978-1-63641-175-0

23 24 25 26 27 — 9 8 7 6 5 4 3 2 1
Printed in the United States of America

As I considered the dedication for this manuscript, my first thought was of my three children, Jeremy, Joshua, and Jennifer. Miracles are gifts from God. Answers to prayers. Blessings and breakthroughs. That is what you are to me—miracles.

I have received love, encouragement, and joy from each of you. It is with a heart of gratitude that I thank God for my miracles. You are my gift from above.

CONTENTS

Acknowledgments xiv

Introduction 1

Week 1:
Miracles in the Lives of Moses, Joshua, and Hannah

DAY 01
CREATION 23
Fasting for a Clean Heart 30

DAY 02
TALKING BUSHES. 37
Fasting for Intimacy With God 44

DAY 03
CROSSING SEAS .51
Fasting for Faith. 58

DAY 04
BREAD FROM HEAVEN 65
Fasting for Forgiveness 72

DAY 05
WALLS FALL DOWN 79
Fasting for Favor 86

DAY 06
THE SUN STANDS STILL 93
Fasting for Protection. 100

DAY 07
NEW LIFE. 107
Fasting for Brokenness. 114

Week 2:
Miracles in the Lives of
Elijah and Elisha

DAY 08
FLOUR AND OIL. 121
Fasting for Consecration 128

DAY 09
LIFE RESTORED. 135
Fasting for Repentance 142

DAY 10
THE HEAVENS OPEN UP 149
Fasting and Confession 156

DAY 11
A DOUBLE PORTION. 163
Fasting for a Double Blessing 170

DAY 12

OIL THAT DOESN'T RUN OUT 177
Fasting for Good Choices. 184

DAY 13

TAKE THE PLUNGE. 191
Fasting for Revelation 198

DAY 14

OPEN EYES. 205
Fasting to Express Grief. 212

Week 3:
Miracles in the Lives of Jesus and
His Disciples

DAY 15

WATER INTO WINE. 219
Fasting for Purity 226

DAY 16

RISE AND WALK 233
Fasting for Patience 240

DAY 17

WIND AND WAVES 247
Fasting for Clarity and Strength. 254

DAY 18
RAISING THE DEAD 261
Fasting for Healing 268

DAY 19
FEEDING THE MULTITUDES 275
Fasting for Humility 282

DAY 20
UNCAGED 289
Fasting for Freedom 296

DAY 21
RESURRECTION 303
Fasting for Peace 310

Miracle Testimonies 316

Final Thoughts 319

Notes 321

About the Author 322

ACKNOWLEDGMENTS

I WOULD LIKE TO acknowledge the following people who have made this book possible.

Lori DeAngelo and Lisa Haines, thank you for your friendship and dedication to helping me edit this book. You have always been there for me.

Diane Campos, thank you for your eye for detail and passion and love for the Lord Jesus Christ. You truly are a gift.

Phil Hotsenpiller, my wonderful husband, you have been my greatest encourager. Thank you for always challenging me.

Influence Church, you are the reason I am where I am today. My prayer and fasting life have grown because of you.

Charisma House, it has been an honor and a privilege to work with you. Your professionalism and commitment to this project have been a blessing to me.

mir·a·cle | ˈmɪrək(ə)l |

noun

an extraordinary event manifesting divine intervention in human affairs.[1]

Have you ever heard someone say, "It would take a miracle for that to happen," or "I hope you believe in miracles because that's the only way you will ever see that happen"?

In a national survey conducted by the Barna Group, half of US adults said they believe the miracles of the Bible happened as they are described. But generationally, the decline in belief was sharp: the numbers were significantly lower among millennials (ages eighteen to thirty) compared to older adults (ages fifty to sixty-eight), with 43 percent and 55 percent, respectively, believing the miracles in Scripture actually happened. When asked whether miracles are possible today, two out of three Americans (67 percent) said yes, with only 15 percent saying no. The others weren't sure. There were again generational differences, with young adults less likely (61 percent) to believe than baby boomers (73 percent).[2]

What precisely do we mean when we talk about miracles? Broadly speaking, miracles are divine interruptions into human affairs. Miracles are beyond our reach, our ability, our effort, our capacity, our strength. They are "beyond human" and beyond our human capacity to reason; thus, they are divine.

While some people relegate miracles to extraordinary saints, the super-special, or the realm of

1

mythology, I think we've all experienced miracles from time to time. These are experiences born out of desperation, the things we have believed for, prayed for, and intently asked God for simply because we had nowhere else to go.

These situations lead us to the "God, if You can hear me" kind of prayers, the ones where we say, "I need a miracle." They could range from a marriage in crisis to a child in need, a financial burden, physical pain, or an emotional breakdown. Miracles are, in short, anything you need that is beyond your personal ability to accomplish. They don't always come out of the places of our deepest belief, but of our deepest need. Life happens to you, and you are suddenly acutely aware that you need God—you need a miracle.

I remember the first miracle I experienced—at least, the first one I remember asking God for. Our son was born premature, and things did not look good for him. I was young and in shock. This was *not* how I envisioned my child's birth. As I sat alone in my hospital bed, I cried out to God for a miracle. I needed something

> Broadly speaking, miracles are divine interruptions into human affairs.

beyond human capacity, beyond the skill of a physician, beyond medical science. I needed nothing less than a miracle.

I wonder now if in some strange way God was teaching me to trust Him—to ask Him, to believe Him. Spoiler alert: yes, I did get my miracle from God. But I received so much more than an answer to my prayer, even more than a beautiful, healthy son. I received a divine encounter. I had an experience with faith! It was my first taste of a supernatural exchange between the all-powerful God and me, His expectant child.

The experience was extraordinary, but I do not believe it was uncommon. Miracles are all around us. Each and every day, *someone* is receiving a miracle. The question is, Are you receiving *your* miracle?

The Greek word translated "miracle" is *dunamis* (the root word for dynamite), and it means power.[3] It is one of three main words Scripture uses in reference to the word *miracle*, the others being *sign* and *wonder*. For example, Psalm 77:14 tells us, "You are the God who performs miracles; you display your power among the peoples" (NIV). From a human perspective, a miracle of God is an extraordinary or unnatural event that reveals or confirms a specific message through a mighty work. When humans bear witness to these divine interruptions, inevitably we will talk about them. I love hearing miracle stories. *Miracle* is a word used even beyond people of faith. Honestly, what would Christmas be without *Miracle on 34th Street*?

These stories are universally treasured precisely because on some level we all live with the hope that there is a sovereign God watching over us. Deep down, some part of us knows life is about more than just good luck, getting a break, or even having "favor." It is the deep knowing that there is a supreme being in the universe who hears the hearts and prayers of His children. I, for one, believe in miracles. What would our life be without an encounter with the all-powerful, all-knowing God of eternity?

WHY I BELIEVE IN MIRACLES

I need to be clear from the start that my interest and belief in miracles are not academic or abstract. Over and over again, I have seen God do remarkable things in the lives of those around me that compel me to believe. While I do believe we have a role to play in whether we yield to God and cooperate with His grace, the gifts of God ultimately speak only of the goodness of the giver. God *is* good. I can think of no truer statement than this. The goodness of God that I have experienced time after time grounds my belief in miracles. It is the goodness of God that makes me trust Him and that makes me tell you that you can trust Him too.

I do not believe miracles are for the super-special or super-holy, but I do believe there are ways we can make ourselves more available and open to God's supernatural work, and one of those ways is fasting, which we will return to momentarily. I cannot stress strongly enough that the basis of this book is not human achievement, human willpower, or human fortitude but the goodness of God, which shows us that we can let go of all the things we hold on to and trust Him fully. That is why fasting is such a powerful practice—it is a way of letting go and fully embracing a God who loves us completely!

While the goodness of God is available to us all, I have had some unique experiences of God's miraculous power through our community at Influence Church. Some of those stories I highlight in a brief chapter at the end of this book. But one of the many stories that have become defining for me is connected to our prayer wall. The location of Influence Church is particular: we meet in a former post office that we purchased from the United States Postal Service. Little did we know at the time that this purchase would be key to making our church a house of prayer for all people (Matt. 21:13).

When a visitor enters our lobby, the first thing he or she notices

4

is the large wall of stones that fills the west side of the space. This is our prayer wall, which is filled with thousands of prayer requests wedged between the stones. Dozens of people enter our doors each day expecting to find the post office. Instead, they are greeted by a trained prayer warrior, who invites them to add their prayers to the wall.

On one occasion, two Muslim women came in. When they were invited to add a prayer request to the wall, one of them began to cry, explaining that her sixteen-year-old son had a brain tumor and his prognosis was not good. She placed her request in the wall and then returned with her friend in a few days to add another request.

Two weeks after that, they came back and gave our prayer team member a report of praise and thanksgiving. A visit to the doctor and additional tests revealed that the boy's tumor was gone. The women gave praise to Jesus for the miracle and the prayer wall. They explained that as Muslims they could not attend our services, but we assured them they were always welcome to pray there and experience the miracle power of Jesus.

We firmly believe the works of God reveal the heart of God and will draw people to true faith in Him. We believe that in some way the presence of God has settled on our prayer wall. It is a touchpoint of faith and a symbol of the miraculous. The moment people enter our building, they sense that God is in our midst. The absence of miracles today is not due to reluctance on God's part but rather a lack of understanding of how God works and a lack of prayer.

What God has done at Influence Church has been a miracle in itself. But beyond that, it seems to me, we are attempting to live out His revealed strategy for the end-time church, one that reveals the goodness of the Father.

THE CONNECTION BETWEEN FASTING AND MIRACLES

Because I believe in a good God, I believe in fasting as one of the primary ways we express our full trust and dependence on Him— and that fasting is a way of leaning into the goodness of God. There is a long-established link between fasting and miracles. Fasting has been part of my personal practice for many years now. I have written workbooks and fasting guides, all in hopes of helping others on their journey. I have personally fasted for breakthrough and power. But when God began to speak to my heart about fasting for miracles, it took me to a new level.

I believe when Jesus said in Matthew 17:21 that some things happen only by prayer and fasting, He meant it. Jesus Himself made the relationship between prayer and fasting explicit. He was teaching us that sometimes we must exercise more than faith to see our miracle. Believing is powerful, and prayer is powerful, but sometimes we must pray, fast, and expect our miracle.

Instead of thinking of miracles as distant, abstract, occasional events that happen for special people in special places, what if you could begin to live a life of miracles—to actually see the super-natural become an everyday occurrence? Fasting is the gateway to this kind of life. Fasting is an act of our will. It is a choice to sup-press the flesh and exercise faith to receive an outcome beyond our ability. We choose to fast when we decide we are hungrier for God and His action than for anything else.

I have heard people argue that fasting is not relevant today, though there are numerous scriptures about fasting in both the Old and New Testaments. I have heard others oversimplify and reduce the role of fasting, arguing that fasting is simply abstaining from food and nothing more. Even some who see merit in fasting contend that it is a physical discipline for the body that has no broader spiritual purpose. But I would disagree.

I believe fasting is a supernatural act of obedience. Jesus Himself fasted for forty days, which prepared Him to encounter the devil's temptation (Luke 4:1–13). The point was not for Jesus to encounter Satan at His "weakest," as if that would somehow heighten the stakes of His test. Yes, His flesh was weak, but His faith was not weak; it was strong, focused, and clear in all the ways only fasting can deepen and clarify our faith. I believe fasting both tempers our flesh and ignites our spirit.

Even though Scripture links fasting and miracles intrinsically, sadly, fasting is not a practice taught in most churches today. Yet Jesus was clear on the subject in Matthew 17:21. Some seasons of our lives are not ordinary and require something more than ordinary faith. Some challenges in your life require more than just prayer. They require more than just asking. They require fasting. Far from a tangential, peripheral act, fasting is practiced throughout the Scriptures by the people of God—from prophets, priests, apostles, and disciples to common men, women, and children. Fasting is an act of obedience to be exercised by all God's children.

WHAT TO EXPECT IN THIS STUDY

There are over 150 miracles in the Bible.[4] Thus highlighting only twenty-one specific miracles was a challenge. All miracle stories in the Bible are important, and all come with intrigue. All reveal the supernatural power of a divine God. But for the purpose of our study, we are going to focus specifically on miracles that illuminate the relationship between miracles and fasting.

Fasting for Miracles has two parts in each day. First we will read and meditate on a miracle passage in Scripture that helps us understand that God still performs miracles in our lives today. Then we will study a fasting passage that demonstrates how God uses fasting to bring about our miracles.

I assume you picked up this book not out of idle curiosity but because you need a miracle in your life. Maybe you never considered that fasting could open the door to your miracle. Before we delve into these powerful stories, may I be so bold as to ask you a few questions?

What are you praying for?

What are you believing God for at this very moment?

What miracle do you need to see in your life?

I want to encourage you to press in hard over the next twenty-one days—to stay focused and disciplined in your fast and in your faith. Miracles *do* still happen today. The God of miracles is very much alive and very much awake. He hears your cry; He knows your heart. He is your everlasting Father.

> # Fasting—it is a way of letting go and fully embracing a God who loves us completely.

FREQUENTLY ASKED QUESTIONS

A miracle is a divine act of God that transcends human understanding, evoking our sense of awe and wonder. Miracles display the greatness of God, causing humanity to recognize that God is still active in our world today. Before we consider the nature of miracles and their relationship to fasting more in-depth, let's begin with some questions and answers to establish a foundational understanding of how fasting works.

IF I FAST, WILL I GET MY MIRACLE?

We don't fast for miracles as an act of our human will but as an act of faith. I want to be very clear: fasting is not merely about our human willpower or human dedication; it is an act of our obedience, of yielding to a God who is infinitely good and intends good things for us. Again, Jesus' teaching to His disciples was direct.

> However, this kind does not go out except by prayer and fasting.
>
> —MATTHEW 17:21

I have wrestled deeply with the relationship of fasting and miracles for some time. I don't believe that our works or effort turn the heart of God. I do believe, however, that obedience brings the favor of God. I do believe that God desires us to temper our own flesh. He tells us to "not fulfill the lust of the flesh" (Gal. 5:16, MEV). Fasting is a way to battle your flesh. Fasting is a way to teach us to move from the natural to the supernatural, from the physical to the divine. Only God can perform miracles, but fasting is an act of our will that clears space for the things of God.

I believe that often our breakthrough is around the corner. We may have prayed and believed, but have we fasted? Remember again that fasting was not an occasional or incidental feature in Scripture—fasting was a discipline demonstrated in both the Old and the New Testaments.

Fasting shows that we are willing to stay strong and fight the battle of any fleshly desire. We stand strong and believe, with God, for the supernatural.

Through God's chosen means of prayer and fasting, I, for one, have seen God move through the supernatural—through the unexpected. I have seen Him work miracles.

DOES GOD ALWAYS ANSWER OUR REQUESTS?

Yes, God does in fact always hear our requests, and yes, He does answer. Sometimes it takes longer than we would like, and often the answer is not the one we want. But yes, God does answer our requests. Have you ever stopped to think maybe God knows something you don't? Maybe it's not the right timing or a change is needed in your life. Maybe while you say you are waiting on God, God is waiting on *you* to do something before He answers. God is never late and never unaware of our needs. He is perfectly in love with you and knows exactly what you need long before you even ask.

IF I BREAK MY FAST, WILL GOD BE MAD AT ME?

The short answer is *no*. Fasting is not for God; fasting is for you. It is an act of discipline and obedience that you alone benefit from. Fasting puts on notice all the demonic forces that try to keep you from victory. Your fast is *your* weapon of warfare. God doesn't want you to miss the blessings you will experience from following through for your answer and breakthrough, but He is never mad at you for not completing your fast.

WHY SHOULD I FAST?

Because Jesus said that power and victory come through fasting. This is a spiritual discipline that moves the heart of God and brings about answers to your prayer. I know firsthand the power and anointing that come from fasting. The enemy hates it when we get serious with God and learn not to rely on the ability of our flesh!

IS INTERMITTENT FASTING THE SAME AS A SPIRITUAL FAST?

While intermittent fasting is healthy and at times even needed, it does not affect your prayer life or move the heart of God like a spiritual fast does. Remember when Jesus said to the disciples, "But you, when you fast, anoint your head and wash your face" (Matt. 6:17). He was not referring simply to not eating food. The disciples knew this was a spiritual requirement and part of their regular routine. Jesus spoke of fasting because there is power in fasting. There is something beyond the physical realm that unleashes the power of God.

WHAT TO EXPECT FROM YOUR FAST

When you fast, your body detoxifies and eliminates toxins from your system. This can cause mild discomfort such as headaches and irritability during withdrawal from caffeine and sugars. Naturally, you will have hunger pangs and cravings. Instead of denying these basic realities of fasting, cooperate with your body's natural responses by limiting your activity. Take time to rest. Remember, you are exercising a spiritual discipline when you fast. Spend time listening to praise and worship music. Pray as often as you can throughout the day. Get away from the normal distractions as much as possible, and keep your heart and mind fixed on seeking God's face.

BENEFITS OF FASTING

Because of the physiological responses we have to fasting, it is easy to focus on what we are *not doing* during a fast instead of what we *are* doing. The truth is, fasting does so much. As Richard J. Foster notes in *Celebration of Discipline*, "Fasting is feasting"—but we are feasting on the Word of God and the presence of God![5]

1. FASTING HELPS US OVERCOME PERSONAL CHALLENGES AND CONFLICTS.

To get a sense of how fasting helps us overcome our own challenges and conflicts, let's look at a few biblical examples of how fasting helped heroes of the faith, and even Jesus Himself, face their own trials.

Fasting brings a sense of humility as we must rely on God alone (Ps. 35:13; 69:10).

Esther fasted when faced with danger (Est. 4:16).

Ezra fasted for protection (Ezra 8:21–28).

Jehoshaphat fasted in the time of war (2 Chron. 20:3).

Jesus fasted in the wilderness when confronted with the devil (Matt. 4:1–2).

2. FASTING OPENS OUR CONNECTION WITH GOD FOR CLARITY AND COMMUNION.

Jesus told His disciples they would fast when He was physically no longer present (Mark 2:20). When we fast, we open ourselves up to a renewed presence of God.

3. FASTING EMPOWERS US TO WALK IN THE SPIRIT AND LIVE OUT OUR TESTIMONY.

In the Old Testament, we often see people fasting in a time of crisis. In the New Testament, we see Jesus fasting for His calling. We should not only fast during problems, but also as a testimony of God's power and sufficiency in our lives. The prophetess Anna, for example, fasted not because of a conflict but as an act of anticipating God as she stood at the gate waiting to see the Messiah (Luke 2:37).

4. FASTING HELPS US DEFEAT THE DEVIL.

We have already seen how Jesus directly connected fasting to warfare when telling His disciples after they could not cast out a demon: "This kind does not go out except by prayer and fasting" (Matt. 17:21). But the precedence of fasting as a weapon that liberates us from the evil one was already established in the Old Testament. According to Isaiah 58:6, fasting helps to "loose the bonds of wickedness, to undo the heavy burdens, to let the oppressed go free, and [to]...break every yoke" (MEV).

TYPES OF FASTS

We all fast whether we realize it or not. God created us to fast. Let's say you sleep seven to eight hours a night. That is fasting! You have no food intake for several hours. That is why we call our first meal of the day "breakfast"—because we break our fast. When Jesus was speaking to the crowd in Matthew 6:16, He said, "When you fast," not *if* you fast. So fasting is to be an intentional part of our life, a personal discipline and action that we engage in with God.

We are tripart beings made up of body, soul, and spirit. Just as our bodies long for physical food, our spirits long for spiritual food. The act of fasting forces our spirit to rely on God to feed us. In John 4:32, the disciples were concerned because Jesus had not yet eaten, "but He said to them, 'I have food to eat of which you do not know.'" Jesus was teaching them the truth about fasting and the Word of God. Fasting makes us dependent on the resources of God. It causes us to believe God will meet our needs and increases our faith and trust in Him.

ABSOLUTE FAST

There are a few different types of fasts you can practice. The first is an absolute fast, which is sometimes called a full or complete fast. This can either be a fast from food and drink or a fast that includes only water and clear liquids. This is not for everyone. It is an intense and potentially dangerous type of fast, particularly for those with certain health issues. The Bible is clear to say that those who went on this kind of fast were led by God to do so and sustained by Him. Make sure you check with your physician before starting an absolute fast.

That said, there is biblical precedent for an absolute fast. Both Moses and Jesus participated in this kind of fast when they fasted forty days. But let me remind you that this was a supernatural or miraculous fast.

When I [Moses] was gone up into the mount to receive the tables of stone, even the tables of the covenant which the Lord made with you, then I abode in the mount forty days and forty nights, I neither did eat bread nor drink water.

—Deuteronomy 9:9, kjv

Then Jesus, being filled with the Holy Spirit, returned from the Jordan and was led by the Spirit into the wilderness, being tempted for forty days by the devil. And in those days He ate nothing, and afterward, when they had ended, He was hungry.

—Luke 4:1–2

PARTIAL FAST

In a partial fast, you choose certain hours to abstain from food—say, sunup to sundown, or waiting until noon to eat. The times are up to you.

So it was, when I heard these words, that I sat down and wept, and mourned for many days; I was fasting and praying before the God of heaven.

—Nehemiah 1:4

JUICE OR LIQUID FAST

In this fast, you drink mostly fruit and vegetable juices. These are typically done for twenty-one days, and you drink only liquids such as juice, smoothies, coffee, water, and so on.

DANIEL FAST

In this ancient fast, which has become popular in recent years, you refrain from meat, sweets, and bread. You drink water and juice and eat only fruits and vegetables. We see this fast demonstrated in the life of Daniel with a powerful result:

Then Daniel said to the steward, whom the master of the officials had set over Daniel, Hananiah, Mishael, and Azariah, "Please test your servants for ten days, and let them give us vegetables to eat and water to drink."...At the end of ten days their countenances appeared fairer and fatter than all the youths who ate the portion of the king's food....As for these four youths, God gave them knowledge and skill in every branch of learning and wisdom. And Daniel had understanding in all kinds of visions and dreams.

—DANIEL 1:11–12, 15, 17, MEV

I ate no tasty food, no meat or wine entered my mouth, nor did I anoint myself at all until three whole weeks were fulfilled. On the twenty-fourth day of the first month, as I was by the side of the great river which is Tigris, I lifted up my eyes and looked and saw a certain man clothed in linen, whose loins were girded with the fine gold of Uphaz. His body also was like beryl, and his face had the appearance of lightning, and his eyes were like lamps of fire, and his arms and his feet were like the gleam of polished bronze, and the sound of his words like the sound of a tumult. I, Daniel, alone saw the vision, while the men who were with me did not see the vision; but a great quaking fell upon them, so that they fled to hide themselves.

—DANIEL 10:3–7, MEV

OTHER FASTS

You can also fast or abstain from a personal pleasure—social media, television, alcohol, shopping, and so on. These are all good areas to exercise self-discipline. Your fast is personal and should be something God leads you to do. Abstain from whatever God has led you to give up. Those with a medical condition may want to choose this type of fast.

In the Bible, we see several examples of other fasts, including

- fasting from anointing oils (Dan. 10:3) and

- abstaining from sexual relations (Exod. 19:15; 1 Cor. 7:5).

CORPORATE FASTS

Unlike an individual fast, in this fast you join a group of believers to fast and pray for a specific matter. This is the type of fast we do annually as a church. We ask God to do a new work and bring a fresh move of His Spirit in our community. We are invited to participate in a group fast with a specific outcome.

Esther appealed to God's people to come together in a corporate fast for the welfare of the Jewish people:

> Go, gather all the Jews who are present in Shushan, and fast for me; neither eat nor drink for three days, night or day. My maids and I will fast likewise. And so I will go to the king, which is against the law; and if I perish, I perish!
>
> —ESTHER 4:16

ISOLATION OR SEPARATION FASTS

While Jesus did not give us a detailed outline of things we are to abstain from during a fast, He did model isolation, or solitude, as something to truly focus on. Note that while we often only see the wilderness as a negative place, prophets (in the tradition of the prophets) would intentionally seek out the isolation of the wilderness to hear the voice of God more clearly!

> So He Himself often withdrew into the wilderness and prayed.
>
> —LUKE 5:16

DISCLAIMER: Please check with your physician before beginning any fast or changing your diet!

STEPS TO TAKE BEFORE YOUR FAST

1. WRITE WHY YOU ARE FASTING.

Be specific. Why are you fasting? Do you need direction, healing, restoration in your marriage, or guidance concerning a family matter? Are you facing financial difficulties? Are you joining a corporate fast?

2. GET YOURSELF PREPARED.

Ask the Holy Spirit to reveal areas of temptation and weakness. Forgive those who have offended you, and ask forgiveness from those you may have offended. Surrender your life fully to Christ and examine your heart for anything that might hinder you from all God has in store for you, as Paul instructs in Romans 12:1–2.

3. DECIDE WHICH FAST IS RIGHT FOR YOU.

The type of fasting you choose is up to you. You could do an absolute fast in which you only drink liquids, or you may desire to fast like Daniel, who abstained from sweets and meats and drank only water. Remember to use the time you would normally eat to engage in worship, prayer, and Bible reading.

4. EXPECT AN INTIMATE EXPERIENCE WITH GOD.

In the words of Psalm 143:6, "I spread out my hands to You; my soul longs for You like a thirsty land." The psalmist had a deep longing to know the heart of God. Intimacy with God starts with *longing* and then becomes a *lifestyle*. Don't rush your devotion time with God. Make this experience a priority, and allow it to become a discovery of all God has for your life.

THE *FASTING FOR MIRACLES* PROCESS

Each day we will journey together through miracle stories and fasting passages. We will read Scripture and discuss the content. Following is the outline of each day's assignment. Take your time going through each day's activities, and allow God to speak to you. You will be surprised at how much He has to say!

MIRACLE PASSAGE

On each of the twenty-one days, you will read a passage of Scripture about miracles. The purpose is to remind us that God does perform supernatural acts in the lives of His children. This will be a time for you to be encouraged and strengthened in your faith. Be sure to read the entire passage. God's Word is life, and it is power.

MIRACLE STORY

This is where I will make an application for the miracle passage. Take your time in reading each day's insight. Make note of what God is saying to you along the journey. There will be much to glean from the stories.

FASTING PASSAGE

Again, each day you will have a fasting passage to study. We can learn much from those who practiced fasting. Take note of the story told in the passage, and make a personal application for your daily study.

FASTING LESSON

In this section I share my thoughts and some practical suggestions for fasting. Remember, we are asking God to unleash our faith by performing miracles. Fasting is an act of discipline and an offering unto God. Stay strong and focused on your journey.

REFLECTION TIME

This is a time for you to work through your thoughts. The questions are drawn both from the miracle story we studied and the fasting passage for that day. This is where you can get real with God. Be honest about your feelings. This is your story to tell.

CLOSING PRAYER

Prayer is the most powerful form of communication we have. It is greater than our phones, social media, or any other means of having a conversation. Prayer is talking to *God*. Each assignment will end with a prayer. Take time to say the prayer, and make it your own.

JOURNAL ENTRY

Over the next twenty-one days, you will discover new things about God and His plan to release miracles into your life. But you will also discover new things about yourself. At the end of each day there will be a place for you to journal your thoughts and self-discoveries. Use this opportunity to chronicle your journey and the many things God is showing you—both about Himself and yourself!

DAILY COACHING VIDEOS

In daily videos posted at TammyHotsenpiller.com, I will coach you through each day's passages and our prayer time. These accountability videos will keep you grounded as you seek God for wisdom and insight into your miracle.

MY DECLARATION

Take a moment now to reflect on what you are believing God for through these twenty-one days. After you answer the following questions, make your declaration and commitment to God. This is a personal and powerful experience of connecting with God before the journey begins.

What miracle are you asking God for over the next twenty-one days?

_____

_____

_____

_____

What type of fast are you committing to do over the next twenty-one days?

_____

_____

_____

_____

week one

MIRACLES in the LIVES of MOSES, JOSHUA, and HANNAH

IN OUR FIRST WEEK TOGETHER we will be reading about miracles in the lives of Moses, Joshua, and Hannah. These stories will encourage you in your faith and propel you forward as you continue to expect your miracle.

day
01

CREATION

W HAT BETTER PLACE to start our journey than at the beginning with the story of creation.

SCRIPTURE READING

In the beginning God created the heavens and the earth. The earth was without form, and void; and darkness was on the face of the deep. And the Spirit of God was hovering over the face of the waters.

Then God said, "Let there be light"; and there was light. And God saw the light, that it was good; and God divided the light from the darkness. God called the light Day, and the darkness He called Night. So the evening and the morning were the first day.

Then God said, "Let there be a firmament in the midst of the waters, and let it divide the waters from the waters." Thus God made the firmament, and divided the waters which were under the firmament from the waters which were above the firmament; and it was so. And God called the firmament Heaven. So the evening and the morning were the second day.

Then God said, "Let the waters under the heavens be gathered together into one place, and let the dry land appear"; and it was so. And God called the dry land Earth, and the gathering together of the waters He called Seas. And God saw that it was good.

Then God said, "Let the earth bring forth grass, the herb that yields seed, and the fruit tree that yields fruit according to its kind, whose seed is in itself, on the earth"; and it was so. And the earth brought forth grass, the herb that yields seed according to its kind, and the tree that yields fruit, whose seed is in itself according to its kind. And God saw that it was good.[3] So the evening and the morning were the third day.

Then God said, "Let there be lights in the firmament of the heavens to divide the day from the night; and let them be for signs and seasons, and for days and years; and let them be for lights in the firmament of the heavens to give light on the earth"; and it was so. Then God made two great lights: the greater light to rule the day, and the lesser light to rule the night. He made the stars also. God set them in the firmament of the heavens to give light on the earth, and to rule over the day and over the night, and to divide the light from the darkness. And God saw that it was good. So the evening and the morning were the fourth day.

Then God said, "Let the waters abound with an abundance of living creatures, and let birds fly above the earth across the face of the firmament of the heavens." So God created great sea creatures and every living thing that moves, with which the waters abounded, according to their kind, and every winged bird according to its kind. And God saw that it was good. And God blessed them, saying, "Be fruitful and multiply, and fill the waters in the seas, and let birds multiply on the earth." So the evening and the morning were the fifth day.

Then God said, "Let the earth bring forth the living creature according to its kind: cattle and creeping thing and beast of the earth, each according to its kind"; and it was so. And God made the beast of the earth according to its kind, cattle according to its kind, and everything that creeps on the earth according to its kind. And God saw that it was good.

Then God said, "Let Us make man in Our image, according to Our likeness; let them have dominion over the fish of the sea, over the birds of the air, and over the cattle, over all the earth and over every creeping thing that creeps on the earth." So God created man in His own image; in the image of God He created him; male and female He created them.

—GENESIS 1:1–27

> So God created man in His own image;
>
> in the image of God He created him;
>
> male and female He created them.
>
> —GENESIS 1:27

MIRACLE
PASSAGE

EVERYTHING FROM NOTHING

God took nothing and made it into everything simply by the power of His Word. As mentioned in the introduction, the Greek word translated "miracle" is *dunamis*—the root of our English word *dynamite*—and means power. It was the power of God's Word, the power of God's voice, that brought all things into being. It was the "and God said..." that caused everything that was not to become everything that is.

God created the world by the power of His Word, and that was the first miracle.

While others may not view creation as a miracle, I do. God speaking the world into existence, by my definition, is absolutely a miracle!

Making everything from nothing is a miracle. Creating mankind, male and female, was a miracle. Breathing life from the very mouth of God into creation was truly a miracle. But isn't that just like God to breathe life into our dead circumstances, breathe creativity and passion into His children's destiny?

Each morning, we wake up with the expectation of a new day, with hope and passion to do more and be more. This is a gift from God.

I am an entrepreneur. My passion is not only to start new businesses and create new strategies but to help others along the way. This is what brings joy to my soul. That is because I am made in the image of God, with endless capabilities and creativity.

On our first day together, I want you to see that

the first miracle God performed was to make *you*. He performed this miracle so we could have fellowship with Him. The Bible says, "So God created man in His own image; in the image of God, He created him; male and female He created them" (Gen. 1:27). He created him, and He created them male and female. Why? So we, being in God's image, could be creative.

Have you ever stopped to think that the very act of reproduction is an act of creativity? "Be fruitful and multiply" (Gen. 1:28). Those were God's words to Adam and Eve. Why? Because He was teaching them their role in creating something new.

Have you ever taken the time to consider that God created you in His image so you might be creative? God gives us all the ingredients we need to be creative. Now all we need is the faith to believe God will move on our behalf. What has God birthed in you to create, design, invent, develop, or research? How can you help humanity with your knowledge and ability?

God took nothing and made it into everything simply by the power of His Word.

Our first miracle establishes the power of God's Word. Again, it was the power of God's Word—God's voice—that made something out of nothingness. With one voice the triune God spoke the world into existence, and you were part of that plan.

As we ponder our first miracle, let me encourage you to stop right now and thank God for making you in His image. God has so much more for you.

FASTING FOR A CLEAN HEART

FASTING PASSAGES

Say to all the people of the land and the priests, "When you fasted and mourned in the fifth month and in the seventh, for these seventy years, was it for me that you fasted? And when you eat and when you drink, do you not eat for yourselves and drink for yourselves?"

—ZECHARIAH 7:5–6, ESV

Thus says the LORD of hosts: The fast of the fourth month and the fast of the fifth and the fast of the seventh and the fast of the tenth shall be to the house of Judah seasons of joy and gladness and cheerful feasts. Therefore love truth and peace.

—ZECHARIAH 8:19, ESV

FASTING LESSON

We begin today's fasting focus with an unusual portion of Scripture. What was happening in Zechariah's day is not too different from what we experience. The people had made fasting into an idol, a ritual, a habit. They were fasting as a memorial to their past victories. But they were doing so with the wrong attitude.

The fast was being offered with a sense of arrogance. The prophet Zechariah first told the people they needed to show mercy and compassion to

30

others. He said, "Do not oppress the widow or the fatherless, the alien or the poor. Let none of you plan evil in his heart against his brother" (Zech. 7:10). Zechariah needed to confront the Israelites about their reason for fasting in the first place. The motive of their heart was being examined.

Today's miracle story reminded us that we have the ability to create. We can create not only ideas and passions but also memories and memorials. In the Zechariah passages, we find God's children idolizing the wrong thing. It is only with a pure heart and the right motive that we can offer our fast before God. Let's start today by examining the motives of our hearts.

Fasting is a gift we offer God by faith. It is true that by our action and discipline we are asking God to meet our request and answer our prayers. But our fast must be done with a pure motive and a clean heart.

> God took nothing and made it into everything simply by the power of His Word.

REFLECTION TIME

What is something you have dreamed about or thought about but never taken the steps to act on? A book? A business? A relationship? God wants you to create. Are you ready to get started? Share something God has given you a passion and desire to accomplish.

_____

_____

_____

_____

Do you have a healthy self-image? I don't mean arrogant or prideful but rather confident and respectful. Almighty God created you in His image for good works. Ephesians 2:10 tells us, "For we are His workmanship, created in Christ Jesus for good works, which God prepared beforehand that we should walk in them."

Take a moment now and write how you feel about yourself. If your self-image needs correction, allow God to speak His words of wisdom and affirmation into your life today.

_____

_____

_____

_____

In our fasting passage today, we read that the Israelites had made fasting into an idol, something they took pride in. God desires a clean heart and a right motive before Him. As you start your fast today, ask yourself if there is any wrong or unclean attitude in your heart. God wants to answer your request. He wants to work a miracle in your life. But He will never compromise His character to do so. Take a moment and examine your heart before God. Write anything that might distract you over the next several days as you enter your fast. Ask God to guard you from anything that would keep you from your miracle.

_____

_____

_____

_____

_____

_____

_____

_____

_____

CLOSING PRAYER

Dear Lord, You are the Creator God, and You made me in Your image. I ask that You reveal Your plan and purpose for my life today. Give me the faith and strength to trust You to perform miracles in my life. I ask for insight, wisdom, and revelation to walk in obedience and become the person You created me to be. In Jesus' name, amen.

JOURNAL ENTRY

_____

_____

_____

_____

_____

_____

_____

_____

_____

day
02

TALKING BUSHES

Today we will look at one of the best-known miracles in the Old Testament: Moses at the burning bush.

SCRIPTURE READING

Now Moses was tending the flock of Jethro his father-in-law, the priest of Midian. And he led the flock to the back of the desert, and came to Horeb, the mountain of God. And the Angel of the LORD appeared to him in a flame of fire from the midst of a bush. So he looked, and behold, the bush was burning with fire, but the bush was not consumed. Then Moses said, "I will now turn aside and see this great sight, why the bush does not burn."

So when the Lord saw that he turned aside to look, God called to him from the midst of the bush and said, "Moses, Moses!" And he said, "Here I am." Then He said, "Do not draw near this place. Take your sandals off your feet, for the place where you stand is holy ground." Moreover He said, "I am the God of your father—the God of Abraham, the God of Isaac, and the God of Jacob." And Moses hid his face, for he was afraid to look upon God.

And the LORD said: "I have surely seen the oppression of My people who are in Egypt, and have heard their cry because of their taskmasters, for I know their sorrows. So I have come down to deliver them out of the hand of the Egyptians, and to bring them up from that land to a good and large land, to a land flowing with milk and honey, to the place of the Canaanites and the Hittites and the Amorites and the Perizzites and the Hivites and the Jebusites. Now therefore, behold, the cry of the children of Israel has come to Me, and I have also seen the oppression with which the Egyptians oppress them. Come now, therefore, and I will send you to Pharaoh that you may bring My people, the children of Israel, out of Egypt." But Moses said to God, "Who am I that I should go to Pharaoh, and that I should bring the children of Israel out of Egypt?"

So He said, "I will certainly be with you. And this shall be a sign to you that I have sent you: When you have brought the people out of Egypt, you shall serve God on this mountain." Then Moses said to God, "Indeed, when I come to the children of Israel and say to them, 'The God of your fathers has sent me to you,' and they say to me, 'What is His name?' what shall I say to them?" And God said to Moses, "I Am Who I Am." And He said, "Thus you shall say to the children of Israel, 'I Am has sent me to you.'" Moreover God said to Moses, "Thus you shall say to the children of Israel: 'The Lord God of your fathers, the God of Abraham, the God of Isaac, and the God of Jacob, has sent me to you. This is My name forever, and this is My memorial to all generations.'"

—Exodus 3:1–15

The fires of life often prove to be the testing ground for our miracle.

"

And the Angel of the LORD appeared to him in a flame of fire from the midst of a bush. So he looked, and behold, the bush was burning with fire, but the bush was not consumed. Then Moses said, "I will now turn aside and see this great sight, why the bush does not burn." So when the LORD saw that he turned aside to look, God called to him from the midst of the bush and said, "Moses, Moses!" And he said, "Here I am."

—EXODUS 3:2-4

MIRACLE PASSAGE

BURNED BUT NOT CONSUMED

Talking bushes are not normal—hence, the miracle!

Have you ever been in the desert and witnessed a bush catching fire from the heat? Surely flames igniting around dry vegetation would be nothing strange for Moses, a man familiar with the desert. It was hot and dry, so brush fires were a common occurrence.

I live in Southern California and know all too well that within a moment a little spark can start a dangerous fire. But this bush was different because it was not consumed. God was *in* the fire. As Moses approached the bush to see this strange occurrence, he heard a voice. Could things get any stranger? Could the voice be real?

It was not just the voice that startled Moses but the power behind the voice. For this voice was the voice of God: "Take your sandals off your feet, for the place where you stand is holy ground" (v. 5). God was *in* the bush. God was in the miracle for this was an encounter with the living God.

Moses was getting ready to see the true manifestation of God. He was getting ready to receive his assignment.

Miracles often come in strange packages. It may be a prompting in your spirit or a confirmation through prayer, but God always finds a way to get our attention.

Have you ever looked back on something and said, "I think God was really trying to get my attention"?

You may not have a burning bush experience, but God still wants to speak with you. As He did for Moses, God wants to give you your kingdom assignment. He wants to give you your miracle.

We all go through the fires of life. Difficulties and setbacks confront us all. I am reminded of a similar miracle story where God was in another fire with three Hebrew boys who would not bow to an evil king.

In Daniel 3, Shadrach, Meshach, and Abed-Nego stood strong in their faith when King Nebuchadnezzar signed an edict ordering everyone to bow before a golden image of him. The three young Hebrews refused to obey, telling the king, "O Nebuchadnezzar, we have no need to answer you in this matter. If that is the case, our God whom we serve is able to deliver us from the burning fiery furnace, and He will deliver us from your hand, O king" (vv. 16–17).

A lot of times we hope God does something miraculous before our lives get uncomfortable. But He doesn't always work that way. Shadrach, Meshach, and Abed-Nego weren't spared the fire. They were tossed into a blaze so hot the men who cast them inside were burned to death.

But Nebuchadnezzar said, "Look!...I see four men loose, walking in the midst of the fire; and they are not hurt, and the form of the fourth is like the Son of God" (v. 25). The king ordered the men to come out of the furnace, and when they did, not even their hair had been singed and they didn't smell like smoke—"the fire had no power" (v. 27)!

This is how it is when we're walking with God. The fires of life often prove to be the testing ground for our miracle.

FASTING FOR INTIMACY WITH GOD

FASTING PASSAGE

So he was there with the LORD forty days and forty nights. He neither ate bread nor drank water. And he wrote on the tablets the words of the covenant, the Ten Commandments.

—EXODUS 34:28, ESV

FASTING LESSON

God loves to talk with His children. For Moses, it began with a burning bush and then continued throughout his lifetime with many other encounters. But one very significant experience took place when Moses was on Mount Sinai receiving the Ten Commandments of God (for the second time, I might add).

The first time did not go so well for him. But there he was again, having an encounter with God.

The Bible tells us Moses received personal instructions from God on how His children should function in life. It was a divine download from God to Moses for humanity. They were the instructions on how to live an obedient and healthy life. The tablets were the very Law of God.

I love the way the Word of God lays out this intimate conversation. The Bible tells us Moses did not eat or drink for forty days while he received the instructions from the Lord. The fact that he received this revelation while on a fast cannot be incidental. His food was the very presence of God.

44

Nothing else could satisfy his longing. If you have ever encountered the power of God's presence, then you know firsthand that all earthly things fade away when you're with Him.

After that encounter Moses made his way down the mountain to give the Law to the children of Israel. The Bible says Moses did not know his face was glowing from being in the presence of God. But the people saw it and were immediately afraid. There was something powerful about the presence of God flowing from Moses' countenance.

In the Book of Acts we read the account of Stephen as he was being stoned to death for his faith. He too had an encounter with God that caused his face to shine like that of an angel:

> And all who sat in the council, looking steadfastly at him, saw
> his face as the face of an angel.
>
> —Acts 6:15

Being in the presence of God is life changing. The more time you spend with God, the more you will radiate His glory.

Whether you are fasting for twenty-one days or forty days, you are having a divine encounter. People *will* begin to see the presence of God on you. He is preparing you for your miracle.

REFLECTION TIME

Moses heard God speaking through a bush, and then he heard Him again when he received the Ten Commandments on Mount Sinai. Have you ever heard God speak to you? Maybe it was not an audible voice but a prompting, a nudging, or a confirmation that let you know God was speaking to you. Share your experience.

_____

_____

_____

_____

Encounters with God should be the norm in our lives. God desires to have an ongoing relationship with His children. Have you ever sensed the presence of God, maybe through an answered prayer or a specific Scripture passage? What was your experience like?

_____

_____

_____

_____

Moses did not eat for forty days and nights while he was in the presence of God on the mountain. He was being sustained by the power of God. As we begin our

twenty-one-day fast, take a moment and revisit your
fasting commitment to God. What are you fasting from?
What does your daily routine look like?

_____

_____

_____

_____

_____

_____

_____

_____

_____

_____

_____

_____

_____

_____

CLOSING PRAYER

Dear Lord, thank You for hearing my prayer and caring about my request. Your plans are perfect and Your ways divine. Give me the strength to stay on my fast and honor my commitment to You. I ask that You meet me in supernatural ways and teach me to go deeper with You, Holy Spirit. In Jesus' name, amen.

JOURNAL ENTRY

day 03

CROSSING
SEAS

TODAY WE WILL look at a critical miracle in the story of the children of Israel's exodus from Egypt: the parting of the Red Sea.

SCRIPTURE READING

Now it was told the king of Egypt that the people had fled, and the heart of Pharaoh and his servants was turned against the people; and they said, "Why have we done this, that we have let Israel go from serving us?" So he made ready his chariot and took his people with him. Also, he took six hundred choice chariots, and all the chariots of Egypt with captains over every one of them. And the LORD hardened the heart of Pharaoh king of Egypt, and he pursued the children of Israel; and the children of Israel went out with boldness. So the Egyptians pursued them, all the horses and chariots of Pharaoh, his horsemen and his army, and overtook them camping by the sea beside Pi Hahiroth, before Baal Zephon.

And when Pharaoh drew near, the children of Israel lifted their eyes, and behold, the Egyptians marched after them. So they were very afraid, and the children of Israel cried out to the Lord. Then they said to Moses, "Because there were no graves in Egypt, have you taken us away to die in the wilderness? Why have you so dealt with us, to bring us up out of Egypt? Is this not the word that we told you in Egypt, saying, 'Let us alone that we may serve the Egyptians'? For it would have been better for us to serve the Egyptians than that we should die in the wilderness."

And Moses said to the people, "Do not be afraid. Stand still, and see the salvation of the LORD, which He will accomplish for you today. For the Egyptians whom you see today, you shall see again no more forever. The LORD will fight for you, and you shall hold your peace."

And the LORD said to Moses, "Why do you cry to Me? Tell the children of Israel to go forward. But lift up your rod, and stretch out your hand over the sea and divide it. And the children of Israel shall go on dry ground through the midst of the sea. And I indeed will harden the hearts of the Egyptians, and they shall follow them. So I will gain honor over Pharaoh and over all his army, his chariots, and his horsemen. Then the Egyptians shall know that I am the LORD, when I have gained honor for Myself over Pharaoh, his chariots, and his horsemen."

And the Angel of God, who went before the camp of Israel, moved and went behind them; and the pillar of cloud went from before them and stood behind them. So it came between the camp of the Egyptians and the camp of Israel. Thus it was a cloud and darkness to the one, and it gave light by night to the other, so that the one did not come near the other all that night.

Then Moses stretched out his hand over the sea; and the LORD caused the sea to go back by a strong east wind all that night, and made the sea into dry land, and the waters were divided. So the children of Israel went into the midst of the sea on the dry ground, and the waters were a wall to them on their right hand and on their left. And the Egyptians pursued and went after them into the midst of the sea, all Pharaoh's horses, his chariots, and his horsemen.

—EXODUS 14:5–23

" Then Moses stretched out his hand over the sea; and the Lord caused the sea to go back by a strong east wind all that night, and made the sea into dry land, and the waters were divided. So the children of Israel went into the midst of the sea on the dry ground, and the waters were a wall to them on their right hand and on their left. And the Egyptians pursued and went after them into the midst of the sea, all Pharaoh's horses, his chariots, and his horsemen.

—Exodus 14:21-23

MIRACLE PASSAGE

PARTING THE WATER

If you have seen the movie *The Ten Commandments* starring Charlton Heston, you are familiar with this passage. (If you haven't seen the film, I highly recommend it!)

Most of us know the story: The Israelites were under the bondage of Pharaoh, king of Egypt. They were being forced into slavery, but Moses knew God had more for His children. Moses' backstory is one of God's providence. When Moses received the word from God to go back and tell Pharaoh to let God's people go, he knew it was a call on his life.

After the ten plagues fell on the Egyptians, Pharaoh had had enough. "Get these people out of my sight," he demanded. But upon further consideration, he realized he had just lost his slaves—his craftsmen and workers. "Go after them," he commanded.

Now, put yourself in the Israelites shoes: These had been your commanders, your leaders, your bosses. You had been under their thumb. They had been watching every move and decision you made. But suddenly you are free. As you leave Egypt and go into the wilderness, you find yourself at a crossroads. The Red Sea is in front of you, mountains are on both sides of you, and the Egyptian army is behind you. The only thing for you to do is curse Moses for convincing you to participate in this insane idea.

Yet God had a plan. God always has a plan.

God told Moses to march forward, lift his staff, and part the Red Sea. Then He commanded the children of Israel to walk across—and they did because they were walking on dry land. As the sea was parted and held back by the power of God, the Israelites crossed in confidence and victory.

As the last person stepped foot on the shore's edge, God commanded Moses to lower his staff, and the water fell back into place. Watching the Egyptians drown was indeed a miraculous sight for these former captives.

We serve a God of miracles. He is able to part your raging seas and lead you through any storm. He will protect you from all enemies that surround you.

God gave them a strategy to win the battle, but it looked different from what they thought it would.

FASTING FOR FAITH

FASTING PASSAGES

Then Jehoshaphat was afraid and set his face to seek the LORD, and proclaimed a fast throughout all Judah.

—2 CHRONICLES 20:3, ESV

Then the Spirit of the LORD came upon Jahaziel the son of Zechariah, the son of Benaiah, the son of Jeiel, the son of Mattaniah, a Levite of the sons of Asaph, in the midst of the assembly. And he said, "Listen, all you of Judah and you inhabitants of Jerusalem, and you, King Jehoshaphat! Thus says the Lord to you: 'Do not be afraid nor dismayed because of this great multitude, for the battle is not yours, but God's. Tomorrow go down against them. They will surely come up by the Ascent of Ziz, and you will find them at the end of the brook before the Wilderness of Jeruel. You will not need to fight in this battle. Position yourselves, stand still and see the salvation of the LORD, who is with you, O Judah and Jerusalem!' Do not fear or be dismayed; tomorrow go out against them, for the LORD is with you."

—2 CHRONICLES 20:14–17

FASTING LESSON

Once again we see an enemy army pursuing God's children. These enemies were coming from the water to do battle with Jehoshaphat. There was

58

only one thing he could do: cry out to God and call the people to fast.

Jehoshaphat knew God was able to protect and provide for the Israelites, yet he decreed a time of prayer and fasting for the people. Fasting was an act of obedience and faith. Fear had swept in like a flood. Jehoshaphat told the people they had no power against this great multitude coming against them, nor did they even know what to do. But he reminded them that their eyes were to be upon the Lord.

Fasting has a way of giving us direction and strength.

Even as Jehoshaphat spoke to the people, his confidence grew.

Jehoshaphat reminded the children of Israel that the God of heaven was also the God who ruled the kingdoms and nations of the earth—that His hand was more powerful and that He was able to withstand any army. As the Israelites fasted and prayed, God indeed performed a miracle.

The Bible tells us that the Spirit of the Lord came upon the men in the assembly and instructed them to go down to the enemy armies and watch God perform a miracle. Speaking for the Lord, the prophet Jahaziel said, "Do not fear or be dismayed; tomorrow, go out against them, for the Lord is with you" (v. 17).

God gave them a strategy to win the battle, but it looked different from what they thought it would.

Stand still and see the Lord move. As the Israelites praised and worshipped the Lord, the armies began to turn on one another— enemy against enemy. God's people continued to stand still and sing praises to the Lord.

God did what He said He would do: He protected them through the storm and provided for them in the war. Fasting gave them God's direction and a divine plan for their safety.

REFLECTION TIME

There are those who believe the parting of the Red Sea was just a biblical exaggeration—that there is no way a raging sea could split wide open upon Moses' command and the lifting of his anointed staff. But I'm sure they also don't believe in miracles generally. My question for you today is, Do *you* believe in miracles? Take a moment and write your faith declaration to God. In your own words, tell Him you believe in miracles and that you are expecting to see Him work in your life over these twenty-one days.

_____

_____

_____

_____

The enemy army was in hot pursuit of Moses and the Israelites. I imagine they looked back once or twice in the process of crossing the sea on dry land. "How close are they?" they must have asked. Yet God remained faithful. There are times in our lives when our enemies seem closer than we'd like. Think of a time when God came through just in the nick of time. The miracle was not just the parting of the Red Sea but also the Lord's protection of and provision for His children. Share your miracle testimony.

_____

_____

_____

_____

Today we read about Jehoshaphat and how he called the
people to a fast for wisdom and God's protection. There
are times when we need clear direction and divine encounters to get through a difficult situation. Fasting can bring
clarity and insight from God. What are you hoping to see
God do in your life over these three weeks? Take some
time and write your prayer request to God.

_____

_____

_____

_____

_____

_____

_____

_____

_____

_____

CLOSING PRAYER

Dear Lord, teach me to hear Your voice and rely on Your will for my life. I ask that You work miracles in my life and help me to boldly testify of Your goodness. I ask that my fast be an offering unto You as a sign of my faith in Your ability to do the supernatural in my life. In Jesus' name, amen.

JOURNAL ENTRY

day
04

BREAD FROM HEAVEN

WHILE IN THE wilderness, the Israelites began to complain that they didn't have enough to eat. Today we will read of how God miraculously provided food for them in the form of manna from heaven.

SCRIPTURE READING

Then the LORD said to Moses, "Behold, I will rain bread from heaven for you. And the people shall go out and gather a certain quota every day, that I may test them, whether they will walk in My law or not. And it shall be on the sixth day that they shall prepare what they bring in, and it shall be twice as much as they gather daily."

Then Moses and Aaron said to all the children of Israel, "At evening you shall know that the LORD has brought you out of the land of Egypt. And in the morning you shall see the glory of the LORD; for He hears your complaints against the LORD. But what are we, that you complain against us?" Also Moses said, "This shall be seen when the LORD gives you meat to eat in the evening, and in the morning bread to the full; for the LORD hears your complaints which you make against Him. And what are we? Your complaints *are* not against us but against the LORD."

Then Moses spoke to Aaron, "Say to all the congregation of the children of Israel, 'Come near before the LORD, for He has heard your complaints.'" Now it came to pass, as Aaron spoke to the whole congregation of the children of Israel, that they looked toward the wilderness, and behold, the glory of the LORD appeared in the cloud.

And the LORD spoke to Moses, saying, "I have heard the complaints of the children of Israel. Speak to them, saying, 'At twilight you shall eat meat, and in the morning you shall be filled with bread. And you shall know that I am the LORD your God.'"

So it was that quail came up at evening and covered the camp, and in the morning the dew lay all around the camp.

And when the layer of dew lifted, there, on the surface of the wilderness, was a small round substance, as fine as frost on the ground. So when the children of Israel saw it, they said to one another, "What is it?" For they did not know what it was. And Moses said to them, "This is the bread which the LORD has given you to eat. This is the thing which the LORD has commanded: 'Let every man gather it according to each one's need, one omer for each person, according to the number of persons; let every man take for those who are in his tent.'"...

And the house of Israel called its name Manna. And it was like white coriander seed, and the taste of it was like wafers made with honey. Then Moses said, "This is the thing which the LORD has commanded: 'Fill an omer with it, to be kept for your generations, that they may see the bread with which I fed you in the wilderness, when I brought you out of the land of Egypt.'"

—EXODUS 16:4-16, 31-32

> Then the LORD said to Moses, "Behold, I will rain bread from heaven for you. And the people shall go out and gather a certain quota every day, that I may test them, whether they will walk in My law or not. And it shall be on the sixth day that they shall prepare what they bring in, and it shall be twice as much as they gather daily."
>
> —EXODUS 16:4-5

MIRACLE PASSAGE

MIRACLE MANNA

Have you ever been hungry—I mean, *really* hungry? I can't even imagine what it must have been like for the Israelites to leave everything they knew to pursue a new home and travel through a seemingly endless wilderness, all the while wondering where their next meal would come from.

We are on day 4 of our fast, so you might be able to relate to the hunger they felt. But relating to their hunger pangs is one thing; actually relying on God for a miracle is quite another. This story is not only about the fact that God supernaturally provided quail and manna each day but also that He was with them every step of the way. The truth is that God is with you each and every day.

The more I study the miracle stories of the Bible, the more I realize how much God wants to perform miracles in our lives. Often our miracles come in the midst of a crisis, when we have nowhere else to go but God. Desperation causes us to be open to God's presence and provision in ways we could not have imagined before.

We also become open to God's work in surprising ways. When the Israelites saw the manna, they were bewildered. Their first question was, *"What is it?"* They had never seen bread like this. Maybe your miracle too will look different from what you expected—maybe it will come in a form that surprises you. Maybe you will ask God, *"What is it?"* But along the journey, you will see that God not only has answered your request but also given you more than you could have ever imagined.

Every miracle starts with a need. It would not be a miracle if we could do it on our own. God has manna in store for us. But we must trust Him daily for our provision. God's desire is that we would walk each day dependent on His provision and His resources.

I love the way the story ends. God commanded Moses to keep a sample of the manna for future generations to see so they would always know God fed the Israelites in the wilderness. God wants us to remember our miracles too and tell them to the next generation.

> # Desperation causes us to be open to God's presence and provision in ways we could not have imagined before.

FASTING FOR FORGIVENESS

FASTING PASSAGE

Now the word of the LORD came to Jonah the second time, saying, "Arise, go to Nineveh, that great city, and preach to it the message that I tell you." So Jonah arose and went to Nineveh, according to the word of the LORD. Now Nineveh was an exceedingly great city, a three-day journey in extent. And Jonah began to enter the city on the first day's walk. Then he cried out and said, "Yet forty days, and Nineveh shall be overthrown!"

So the people of Nineveh believed God, proclaimed a fast, and put on sackcloth, from the greatest to the least of them. Then word came to the king of Nineveh; and he arose from his throne and laid aside his robe, covered himself with sackcloth and sat in ashes. And he caused it to be proclaimed and published throughout Nineveh by the decree of the king and his nobles, saying, Let neither man nor beast, herd nor flock, taste anything; do not let them eat, or drink water.

But let man and beast be covered with sackcloth, and cry mightily to God; yes, let every one turn from his evil way and from the violence that is in his hands. Who can tell if God will turn and relent, and turn away from His fierce anger, so that we may not perish? Then God saw their works, that they turned from their evil way; and God relented from the disaster that He had said He would bring upon them, and He did not do it.

—JONAH 3:1–10

FASTING LESSON

Most of us know about Jonah because of the whale, but there is so much more to the story. It's not just about a man being swallowed by a whale for God to get his attention. It's also the story of a group of people, the Ninevites, who were opposed to God and His ways.

Jonah did not like the Ninevites. He actually would have been quite happy if God destroyed them. But as it turns out for most of us who hope for the destruction of our enemies, that was not his assignment. Jonah was not called to destroy the Ninevites but to preach to them. His assignment was to tell them to repent—to turn to God and forsake their unrighteousness.

Much to Jonah's surprise, they did.

The king called for fasting and repentance, and God heard the cry of the Ninevites and forgave them. With love and compassion, He healed a nation.

Jonah was *not* happy.

Fasting has a way of purifying our hearts. This wicked group of people examined their hearts through fasting and repentance and met a genuine and true God.

God calls us to fast for a reason: to show us the true intentions of our hearts. Many of us want a miracle. We asked for a miracle, even believed for a miracle.

But often through the act of fasting, God shows us His plan, His future for us. Yes, God wants to answer our prayers; He wants to give us our miracles. But more importantly, He wants us to come to Him with clean hands and a pure heart. God has good and not evil for you, but that is often clouded by our own desires and preferences.

As you fast today, examine your life and the motives behind your request. Drill deep into your heart. God is doing more than you can even imagine. If you don't see it, ask Him to show you. Remember Paul's words in Ephesians 3:20: God "is able to do exceedingly abundantly above all that we ask or think, according to the power that works in us."

REFLECTION TIME

Complaining is so easy to do. God provides for our daily
needs. But inevitably another crisis comes out of nowhere,
and we begin to doubt God and grumble that He has for-
gotten all about us. Today's passage reminds us that God
cares about our needs and desires. Take a moment and write
your thanks to God for the ways He has provided for you
already, giving you a family, job, health, salvation, friends,
and so on. Counting our blessings helps us remember God is
good and His mercies come every morning.

_____

_____

_____

_____

Sometimes it takes a setback or crisis for us to ask God for
a miracle. We become so comfortable with the status quo
that we fail to see the breakthrough. Think of a time when
God used a setback in your life to work a miracle. Share
your experience.

_____

_____

_____

_____

_____

Today's fasting passage taught us a valuable lesson about ignoring God when He gives us an assignment. Jonah hated the Ninevites more than he feared the voice of God. God's plan was not only to save a nation but to heal a prejudiced heart. Fasting brought an awareness of God's divine plan for Nineveh. Jonah had to learn the hard way. Has your fast revealed any resentful or hateful thing in your life? Ask God to use this fast to show you any hidden hardness you may not even know you have. Take a moment and reflect on what God is showing you.

_____

_____

_____

_____

_____

_____

_____

_____

_____

_____

CLOSING PRAYER

Dear Lord, today I was reminded of Your great provision and pleasure in me as Your child. I ask that You teach me how to grow deeper in my relationship with You. Show me if there is anything in my life I need to confess or repent of. I ask that my fast would be a prayer unto You alone. Thank You for the miracles that are coming my way. In Jesus' name, amen.

JOURNAL ENTRY

_____

_____

_____

_____

_____

_____

_____

_____

_____

_____

day
05

WALLS FALL DOWN

BEFORE ENTERING THE Promised Land, the Jewish people had to overcome a major obstacle: a fortified city called Jericho. Today we will read about how God supernaturally caused Jericho's "impenetrable" walls to fall.

SCRIPTURE READING

Now Jericho was securely shut up because of the children of Israel; none went out, and none came in. And the LORD said to Joshua: "See! I have given Jericho into your hand, its king, and the mighty men of valor. You shall march around the city, all you men of war; you shall go all around the city once. This you shall do six days. And seven priests shall bear seven trumpets of rams' horns before the ark. But the seventh day you shall march around the city seven times, and the priests shall blow the trumpets. It shall come to pass, when they make a long blast with the ram's horn, and when you hear the sound of the trumpet, that all the people shall shout with a great shout; then the wall of the city will fall down flat. And the people shall go up every man straight before him." Then Joshua the son of Nun called the priests and said to them, "Take up the ark of the covenant, and let seven priests bear seven trumpets of rams' horns before the ark of the LORD." And he said to the people, "Proceed, and march around the city, and let him who is armed advance before the ark of the LORD."

So it was, when Joshua had spoken to the people, that the seven priests bearing the seven trumpets of rams' horns before the LORD advanced and blew the trumpets, and the ark of the covenant of the LORD followed them. The armed men went before the priests who blew the trumpets, and the rear guard came after the ark, while the priests continued blowing the trumpets. Now Joshua had commanded the people, saying, "You shall not shout or make any noise with your voice, nor shall a word proceed out of your mouth, until the day I say to you, 'Shout!' Then you shall shout."

So he had the ark of the LORD circle the city, going around it once. Then they came into the camp and lodged in the camp.

And Joshua rose early in the morning, and the priests took up the ark of the LORD. Then seven priests bearing seven trumpets of rams' horns before the ark of the LORD went on continually and blew with the trumpets. And the armed men went before them. But the rear guard came after the ark of the LORD, while the priests continued blowing the trumpets. And the second day they marched around the city once and returned to the camp. So they did six days.

But it came to pass on the seventh day that they rose early, about the dawning of the day, and marched around the city seven times in the same manner. On that day only they marched around the city seven times. And the seventh time it happened, when the priests blew the trumpets, that Joshua said to the people: "Shout, for the LORD has given you the city! Now the city shall be doomed by the LORD to destruction, it and all who are in it. Only Rahab the harlot shall live, she and all who are with her in the house, because she hid the messengers that we sent. And you, by all means abstain from the accursed things, lest you become accursed when you take of the accursed things, and make the camp of Israel a curse, and trouble it. But all the silver and gold, and vessels of bronze and iron, are consecrated to the LORD; they shall come into the treasury of the LORD."

So the people shouted when the priests blew the trumpets. And it happened when the people heard the sound of the trumpet, and the people shouted with a great shout, that the wall fell down flat. Then the people went up into the city, every man straight before him, and they took the city.

—JOSHUA 6:1–20

"

So the people shouted when the priests
blew the trumpets. And it happened
when the people heard the sound of
the trumpet, and the people shouted
with a great shout, that the wall fell
down flat. Then the people went
up into the city, every man straight
before him, and they took the city.

—Joshua 6:20

"

MIRACLE
PASSAGE

A FORTIFIED CITY FALLS

We have read several miracle stories so far—from the creation of humanity to a talking bush, and then the dividing of a sea and God's providing quail and manna in the wilderness.

Today's passage is no different. It is the story of how God fulfilled His promise and gave the city of Jericho to the Israelites. It's also the story of how God saved a harlot named Rahab, who later became part of the genealogy of Jesus. There are so many miracles in the story, but let's focus specifically on the miracle of the Jericho wall.

Jericho was a strong, fortified city situated at the top of a hill so enemies and intruders could be seen from afar and any attempted attack averted. The walls of this great city had withstood storms and adversity from the past—but now God was involved.

God promised that He would give the Israelites the city. Joshua's command was to march around the city one time each day for six days, and then on the seventh day to march around the city seven times. They were then to blow the trumpets and shout unto God as an expression of their faith that God was giving them the victory.

As God had promised, the walls of Jericho came tumbling down as the peopled cried out. Everyone living in the city was destroyed—except Rahab and her household. God did everything He said He would do. But the people had to do their part, which included trusting that Joshua had in fact heard the voice of God.

Yet as it is for all of us, believing God never comes without resistance. I'm sure as they marched around the city each day, insults and assaults were being spewed in their direction from those inside: "Look at these crazy Israelites. Don't they know they have come against a fortified city? We are greater and stronger than they are!"

But when God gives you a word, you must trust that it is true. God said He would give them the city, and He was true to His Word.

You may feel like you are marching around a fortified city—something that's bigger than you, stronger than you, and completely out of your ability to conquer. But when God speaks, His word is true.

What are you believing God for? What miracle do you need?

Think of all the obstacles that have come against you and your miracle as the fortified city of Jericho. Now begin to pray for the walls to come down. March around *your miracle.* Shout, worship, praise, and see the walls come falling down. Your miracle is waiting for you on the other side of the walls.

FASTING FOR FAVOR

FASTING PASSAGE

And Mordecai told them to answer Esther: "Do not think in your heart that you will escape in the king's palace any more than all the other Jews. For if you remain completely silent at this time, relief and deliverance will arise for the Jews from another place, but you and your father's house will perish. Yet who knows whether you have come to the kingdom for such a time as this?"

Then Esther told them to reply to Mordecai: "Go, gather all the Jews who are present in Shushan, and fast for me; neither eat nor drink for three days, night or day. My maids and I will fast likewise. And so I will go to the king, which is against the law; and if I perish, I perish!'"

—ESTHER 4:13–16

FASTING LESSON

If you don't know the story of Queen Esther, go back and start at the beginning of the Book of Esther. Here we find an example of God's power and provision for His people. Esther was a beautiful young Jewish woman who had been divinely appointed by God as queen. It was not her beauty alone that gave her the position; it was divine providence and the favor of God.

As most stories go, there is a villain. Haman was plotting to get rid of God's chosen people, the Jews. He was arrogant and prideful and had a personal vendetta against Esther's cousin Mordecai. The issue had become personal, and eventually his every waking thought was to get rid of the Jews.

Esther knew she needed wisdom and strategy from God. She sent out a decree that all the Jews in the land were to fast for three days and nights and ask God to give her favor as she approached the king with a request. Esther understood that some miracles and answers to prayer come by fasting. Some breakthroughs come by obedience.

The people fasted and prayed—and God moved. God's people were protected, and evil agendas were revealed.

How about you? Are you willing to fast for your breakthrough? Do you have the boldness to stand up for what is right and speak on behalf of others? Miracles happen when we take a bold stand— when we fast and believe God for what we cannot do.

> # As it is for all of us, believing God never comes without resistance.

REFLECTION TIME

The story of Jericho fascinates me. Only a miracle from God could cause such strong and fortified walls to come tumbling down. I believe God gave us this story to teach us that walls in our lives can indeed come down. We must be willing to walk in faith around our obstacles. What are you dealing with right now that appears to be walls keeping you from your miracle?

_____

_____

_____

_____

We will always deal with enemies and discouraging voices in life. Whether it is a physical person or the enemy, negative voices are real. Who or what are you encountering today that you need to ignore?

_____

_____

_____

_____

I love the story of Queen Esther. Maybe it's because I love her faith. She knew there was no hope for the Jews unless God intervened. She used her position to call the people to fast and pray. There are times for personal and private fasting, but there are also times for corporate fasting. Esther called a fast and asked the people to pray so God would give her wisdom and favor as she approached the king. Are you fasting with anyone over this twenty-one-day period? If so, write the names of those joining you and why you chose those individuals. Take some time today and pray with them that God would give you wisdom and favor as you wait for your miracle.

_____

_____

_____

_____

_____

_____

_____

_____

_____

_____

_____

_____

CLOSING PRAYER

Dear Lord, I ask that You protect me from my adversaries and those who wish to bring me harm. Give me the strength and faith to keep marching around my walls until I see them come falling down. Accept my fast today as an act of my faith that You are using to bring my miracle to pass. Thank You for Your love and watchcare. In Jesus' name, amen.

JOURNAL ENTRY

_____

_____

_____

_____

_____

_____

_____

_____

_____

day
06

The SUN STANDS STILL

HAVE YOU EVER wished you could turn back time or at least get an extra hour or two in your day? In today's story God miraculously made the sun and moon stand still until His people had won the victory over their enemy. If you think it's too late for your breakthrough, think again!

SCRIPTURE READING

Now it came to pass when Adoni-Zedek king of Jerusalem heard how Joshua had taken Ai and had utterly destroyed it—as he had done to Jericho and its king, so he had done to Ai and its king—and how the inhabitants of Gibeon had made peace with Israel and were among them, that they feared greatly, because Gibeon was a great city, like one of the royal cities, and because it was greater than Ai, and all its men were mighty. Therefore Adoni-Zedek king of Jerusalem sent to Hoham king of Hebron, Piram king of Jarmuth, Japhia king of Lachish, and Debir king of Eglon, saying, "Come up to me and help me, that we may attack Gibeon, for it has made peace with Joshua and with the children of Israel." Therefore the five kings of the Amorites, the king of Jerusalem, the king of Hebron, the king of Jarmuth, the king of Lachish, *and* the king of Eglon, gathered together and went up, they and all their armies, and camped before Gibeon and made war against it.

And the men of Gibeon sent to Joshua at the camp at Gilgal, saying, "Do not forsake your servants; come up to us quickly, save us and help us, for all the kings of the Amorites who dwell in the mountains have gathered together against us."

So Joshua ascended from Gilgal, he and all the people of war with him, and all the mighty men of valor. And the LORD said to Joshua, "Do not fear them, for I have delivered them into your hand; not a man of them shall stand before you." Joshua therefore came upon them suddenly, having marched all night from Gilgal.

So the Lord routed them before Israel, killed them with a great slaughter at Gibeon, chased them along the road that goes to Beth Horon, and struck them down as far as Azekah and Makkedah. And it happened, as they fled before Israel and were on the descent of Beth Horon, that the Lord cast down large hailstones from heaven on them as far as Azekah, and they died. There were more who died from the hailstones than the children of Israel killed with the sword.

Then Joshua spoke to the Lord in the day when the Lord delivered up the Amorites before the children of Israel, and he said in the sight of Israel: "Sun, stand still over Gibeon; and Moon, in the Valley of Aijalon." So the sun stood still, and the moon stopped, till the people had revenge upon their enemies. Is this not written in the Book of Jasher? So the sun stood still in the midst of heaven, and did not hasten to go down for about a whole day. And there has been no day like that, before it or after it, that the Lord heeded the voice of a man; for the Lord fought for Israel. Then Joshua returned, and all Israel with him, to the camp at Gilgal.

—JOSHUA 10:1–15

> Then Joshua spoke to the LORD in the day when the LORD delivered up the Amorites before the children of Israel, and he said in the sight of Israel: "Sun, stand still over Gibeon; and Moon, in the Valley of Aijalon." So the sun stood still, and the moon stopped, till the people had revenge upon their enemies. Is this not written in the Book of Jasher? So the sun stood still in the midst of heaven, and did not hasten to go down for about a whole day. And there has been no day like that, before it or after it, that the LORD heeded the voice of a man; for the LORD fought for Israel.
>
> —JOSHUA 10:12–14

MIRACLE PASSAGE

GOD PROLONGS A DAY

Some days you just wish you had more time! Maybe you are working outside in the yard or on an outdoor project, and you need the sun to stay up just a *little* longer so you can finish. Or maybe you're spending time with someone you love and wish the day could be extended...

Well, that is exactly what happened to Joshua when he fought the Amorites at Gibeon. God in His divine wisdom knew the Israelites needed more time. He'd already promised to deliver them. He'd commanded Joshua not to fear, for God had delivered the enemy into their hands.

This was one of those times when God wanted the people to see His miracle-working power.

It goes against all scientific knowledge for the sun to stand still. Yet, let's remember who created the sun, moon, and stars—yes, the very One who commanded time to stand still.

Joshua needed more time to fight the battle. Five competent kings had brought their armies to fight against the Israelites. Joshua knew he had the advantage because the enemy was growing weary. But he did not want them to return to their fortified cities and rest. He wanted to take them out in one day.

Hence, he asked God to give him more daylight.

The Israelite army had marched all night from Gilgal to Gibeon, a distance of twenty miles, to battle against their enemy. They were exhausted, but adrenaline was on their side. They did not want to stop for the night. They needed to press through. They needed God to prolong the day.

Causing the sun to stand still is certainly a miracle, but it's not much different from what He often does in the lives of His children.

He prolongs His blessings, His favor, His protection, to give us the advantage. He controls the earth and all that He created.

This is a miracle we can find both hope and confidence in: that God truly does direct our steps each and every day.

FASTING FOR PROTECTION

FASTING PASSAGE

Then I proclaimed a fast there, at the river Ahava, that we might humble ourselves before our God, to seek from him a safe journey for ourselves, our children, and all our goods. For I was ashamed to ask the king for a band of soldiers and horsemen to protect us against the enemy on our way, since we had told the king, "The hand of our God is for good on all who seek him, and the power of his wrath is against all who forsake him." So we fasted and implored our God for this, and he listened to our entreaty.

—EZRA 8:21–23, ESV

FASTING LESSON

God comes through again. In the miracle story we just read, we saw the power of God to extend daylight so the Israelites could finish the battle and defeat their enemy. In our fasting passage today, we read a similar story.

Ezra knew he needed help for safe travels from Israel's enemy, but he did not want to ask the king. He had been bold in declaring the goodness and fame of his God to all the people. He had proclaimed that his God was strong and would protect and guide the people. Now he had to act on his faith. He was too proud to ask the king for help since he'd boasted in God's strength, but this led him to faith.

Ezra called a fast and invited the people to join him in seeking God for their protection and well-being. And then Ezra trusted that God would come through for them.

There are times in our lives when we must simply trust God. We have decreed and declared, we have spoken of His goodness and His power, and now it is time to exercise our faith. Ezra knew God was able to provide for the Israelites, but I think deep down he wanted to ask for help. This is when our faith is tested—when we want to rely on the resources and strength of others but know we must trust in God alone.

It takes a lot of faith and patience to wait on God to move. It's tempting to try to use the resources and connections of others to bring about the miracle we need. We don't often consider that the delay may be precisely what God has arranged to test our faith.

If I may be so bold, let me ask you: Are you fully trusting God for your miracle? Is your fast an act of obedience from a place of faith? Is it an offering you are giving unto God?

Don't be tempted to resort to man's ability to meet your need. You will only shortchange your testimony.

> # There are times in our lives when we must simply trust God.

REFLECTION TIME

Whether it was a sunrise or a sunset, there have been times when I wished the sun would just stand still. God is the Creator of each and every moment, and He knows how to make the most of your day. How are you using the time God gives you? This twenty-one-day fast is a great time to look at your schedule and see if you need to make any adjustments to your calendar. Take some time right now and ask God to show you if you are making the most of your time. He will fight your battles. He can prolong your day! But He also wants us to use good time management. Take a moment and write some ways you could better use your time.

_____

_____

_____

_____

God's ways are beyond our ways. I love the fact that God can turn our enemies against one another to protect us from their harm. God tells us in Exodus 14:14, "The LORD will fight for you, and you shall hold your peace." Whether it is God telling the sun to stand still or telling *you* to stand still, you must take Him at His Word. In what areas do you need to just stop and let God work in your life? List below the areas where you need to pause and let God perfect His will.

_____

_____

_____

_____

Ezra wanted God to work on behalf of the people. He didn't want any assistance from the king. He wanted God to answer his prayer. Faith and fasting were the keys he had to open the door for the Israelites' safe travels. What is something you are believing God for that only He can do? List your "only God" prayer request.

_____

_____

_____

_____

_____

_____

_____

_____

_____

_____

CLOSING PRAYER

Dear Lord, You alone are the Creator of the universe. I trust that Your ways are higher than mine. I ask that You show me how to believe for greater things. Help me not to allow the cares of this world to distract me from Your divine plan. I pray I will boldly declare the works of Your kingdom. In Jesus' name, amen.

JOURNAL ENTRY

_____

_____

_____

_____

_____

_____

_____

_____

_____

day
07

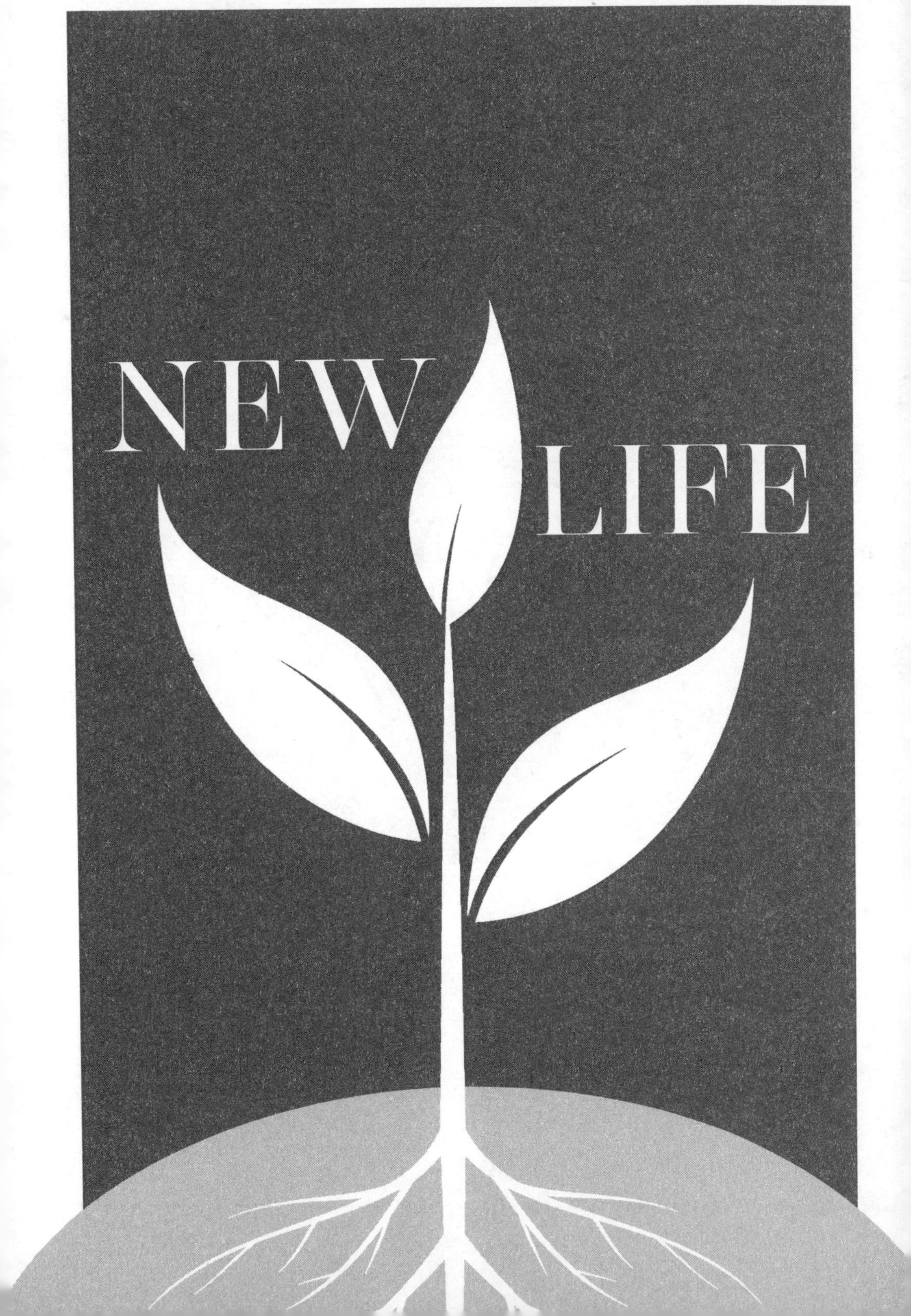
NEW
LIFE

IF YOU'VE EVER wanted something that seemed would never come to pass, you can relate to Hannah. Let the Holy Spirit fill your heart with hope today as you read of how a barren woman miraculously gave birth to one of Scripture's most anointed prophets.

SCRIPTURE READING

Now there was a certain man of Ramathaim Zophim, of the mountains of Ephraim, and his name was Elkanah the son of Jeroham, the son of Elihu, the son of Tohu, the son of Zuph, an Ephraimite. And he had two wives: the name of one was Hannah, and the name of the other Peninnah. Peninnah had children, but Hannah had no children. This man went up from his city yearly to worship and sacrifice to the LORD of hosts in Shiloh. Also the two sons of Eli, Hophni and Phinehas, the priests of the LORD, were there. And whenever the time came for Elkanah to make an offering, he would give portions to Peninnah his wife and to all her sons and daughters. But to Hannah he would give a double portion, for he loved Hannah, although the LORD had closed her womb. And her rival also provoked her severely, to make her miserable, because the LORD had closed her womb. So it was, year by year, when she went up to the house of the LORD, that she provoked her; therefore she wept and did not eat.

Then Elkanah her husband said to her, "Hannah, why do you weep? Why do you not eat? And why is your heart grieved? Am I not better to you than ten sons?"

So Hannah arose after they had finished eating and drinking in Shiloh. Now Eli the priest was sitting on the seat by the doorpost of the tabernacle of the LORD. And she was in bitterness of soul, and prayed to the LORD and wept in anguish.

Then she made a vow and said, "O LORD of hosts, if You will indeed look on the affliction of Your maidservant and remember me, and not forget Your maidservant, but will give Your maidservant a male child, then I will give him to the LORD all the days of his life, and no razor shall come upon his head."

And it happened, as she continued praying before the LORD, that Eli watched her mouth. Now Hannah spoke in her heart; only her lips moved, but her voice was not heard. Therefore Eli thought she was drunk. So Eli said to her, "How long will you be drunk? Put your wine away from you!"

But Hannah answered and said, "No, my lord, I am a woman of sorrowful spirit. I have drunk neither wine nor intoxicating drink, but have poured out my soul before the LORD. Do not consider your maidservant a wicked woman, for out of the abundance of my complaint and grief I have spoken until now."

Then Eli answered and said, "Go in peace, and the God of Israel grant your petition which you have asked of Him."

And she said, "Let your maidservant find favor in your sight." So the woman went her way and ate, and her face was no longer sad.

Then they rose early in the morning and worshiped before the LORD, and returned and came to their house at Ramah. And Elkanah knew Hannah his wife, and the LORD remembered her. So it came to pass in the process of time that Hannah conceived and bore a son, and called his name Samuel, saying, "Because I have asked for him from the LORD."

—1 SAMUEL 1:1–20

> Then they rose early in the morning and worshiped before the LORD, and returned and came to their house at Ramah. And Elkanah knew Hannah his wife, and the LORD remembered her. So it came to pass in the process of time that Hannah conceived and bore a son, and called his name Samuel, saying, "Because I have asked for him from the LORD."
>
> —1 SAMUEL 1:19–20

MIRACLE PASSAGE

A BARREN WOMAN CONCEIVES

Have you ever wanted something so badly, but it seemed God was answering everyone's prayers but yours? That was the case for Hannah. She was blessed to have a husband who loved her dearly, but her heart was still longing for another love—the love of a child.

She had asked the Lord many times for a child, but it seemed He was just not listening. To make matters worse, her husband, Elkanah, had a second wife who had multiple children, and she took great joy in reminding Hannah of her ability to have a family.

Hannah's heart was broken. Each year she made her way to the temple to ask God to open her womb— to bless her with a family, to give her a child.

Often we wonder why God is hesitant or slow to answer our request. I have prayed with many women who have asked God for a baby—women who would make great mothers, women of faith and love and kindness toward others.

I don't understand the delays or, at times, the denials, but I do know that God is a good God, and He has a plan for every one of His children.

Hannah did not stop asking God for her miracle. On a certain occasion as she entered the temple to pray, the priest Eli saw her broken spirit. Her lips were moving in silent prayer as she made her petition to God. Not understanding her pain, Eli confused her brokenness for drunkenness. He rebuked

112

her behavior and called her out. "No, my lord," she replied. "I am not drunk as you suppose. I am a woman of sorrowful spirit."

Eli felt the prompting from the Lord and prophesied over her. He told her to go in peace. Her petition had been granted. A miracle was on the way. Just as Eli prophesied, Hannah became pregnant, and she gave birth to a beautiful baby boy. She named him Samuel, saying it was "because I have asked for him from the LORD" (1 Sam. 1:20).

I do not presume to always understand the ways of God, but there do seem to be patterns and formulas in the Word of God that teach us how to exercise our faith and never give in.

How do we ask God and believe without wavering? Ultimately, the answers to our prayers are in the hands of God. But we don't stop asking, we don't stop seeking, and we don't stop knocking.

Miracles come from the heart of God, and it is His pleasure to meet the needs of His children.

Don't give up on your prayer. Don't stop believing in God for your miracle. We are to expect miracles. One day as I was praying over the words "expect a miracle," God spoke to my heart. In my spirit I heard, "Tammy, your job is to *expect*; My job is to *bring the miracle*."

Let me encourage you, don't ever stop expecting your miracle.

FASTING FOCUS

FASTING FOR BROKENNESS

FASTING PASSAGE

And they said to me, "The survivors who are left from the captivity in the province are there in great distress and reproach. The wall of Jerusalem is also broken down, and its gates are burned with fire." So it was, when I heard these words, that I sat down and wept, and mourned for many days; I was fasting and praying before the God of heaven.

—NEHEMIAH 1:3–4

FASTING LESSON

Nehemiah, a Jewish follower of Yahweh, was a high official in the court of King Artaxerxes during the Babylonian captivity. When he heard that the walls of Jerusalem had fallen, his heart was broken for his people of Israel. This was his homeland. This was God's people. When the king observed Nehemiah's broken spirit, he asked what he could do for him. In response, Nehemiah boldly asked if he could return and rebuild the walls of Jerusalem.

The king witnessed not only a broken spirit but a man convicted to pray and fast for his people.

Often when we are grieving, we do not have a desire for food. But God still sees the motives of our hearts; He sees when our hearts are broken and our spirits are grieved.

Our fast is part of our prayer. It is something we

do as an offering unto God. It is a way to discipline our flesh and seek the things above.

This was the case for Nehemiah. God saw his willingness to serve His people.

As you read the rest of the Book of Nehemiah, you see that God placed a special anointing on this man. I believe Nehemiah practiced fasting as part of a spiritual discipline. God's favor was upon him because of his obedience and pure heart for the things of God.

We follow a good God who loves to bestow good gifts on His children. In the Book of James we read, "Every good gift and every perfect gift is from above, and comes down from the Father of lights, with whom there is no variation or shadow of turning" (Jas. 1:17).

As you fast, remember that others are observing your testimony. Whether you are feeling discouraged, grieved, or simply trusting God for your miracle, present your heart to the Lord. He is the Miracle Worker.

> # Miracles come from the heart of God, and it is His pleasure to meet the needs of His children.

REFLECTION TIME

Have you ever felt that God let you down? Maybe you thought you had done all you knew to do to trust Him yet received no answer. Keep in mind that God's delays are not always denials. What are you asking God for that you have not seen happen yet? As you write your answer, shift from writing a prayer request to declaring what you expect God to do. Expect a miracle!

_____

_____

_____

_____

God gave Hannah her miracle baby, but it took longer than she thought it would. Sometimes our grief is exactly what God will use to bring about both His glory and our answer. Hannah knew she had to go to God in prayer. She poured out her heart to God, and He heard her plea. How does Hannah's example speak to you?

_____

_____

_____

_____

Both Hannah and Nehemiah were broken in spirit. Hannah got the attention of the priest Eli, and Nehemiah got the attention of the king. It's hard to hide our grief. People are always watching us—even in times of heartache, disappointment, or brokenness. But God has a way of using others to answer our requests. Stay dependent on God, but don't be ashamed to share your need. You never know how God will use it. As you fast today, find ways to share your testimony with someone. God may surprise you. Take time to write your thanks to God for His grace and faithfulness to you.

_____

_____

_____

_____

_____

_____

_____

_____

_____

_____

CLOSING PRAYER

Dear Lord, I ask You to forgive me for not trusting You. There have been times when my grief got the best of me and I could not see You working. Teach me to be honest and vulnerable with those around me, and show me how to allow others to be used by You in my life. In Jesus' name, amen.

JOURNAL ENTRY

MIRACLES in the LIVES of ELIJAH and ELISHA

TODAY WE BEGIN WEEK 2 of our twenty-one-day journey. Over the next week I want to introduce you to two Old Testament prophets, Elijah and Elisha, through whom God performed multiple miracles. Each day we will observe the way God met their needs through miracles and faith.

day 08

FLOUR and OIL

IF YOU'VE EVER felt all hope was gone, fasten your seat belt. Today's story about Elijah and the widow at Zarephath is sure to encourage you.

SCRIPTURE READING

Then the word of the LORD came to him, saying, "Arise, go to Zarephath, which belongs to Sidon, and dwell there. See, I have commanded a widow there to provide for you." So he arose and went to Zarephath. And when he came to the gate of the city, indeed a widow was there gathering sticks. And he called to her and said, "Please bring me a little water in a cup, that I may drink." And as she was going to get it, he called to her and said, "Please bring me a morsel of bread in your hand."

So she said, "As the LORD your God lives, I do not have bread, only a handful of flour in a bin, and a little oil in a jar; and see, I am gathering a couple of sticks that I may go in and prepare it for myself and my son, that we may eat it, and die."

And Elijah said to her, "Do not fear; go and do as you have said, but make me a small cake from it first, and bring it to me; and afterward make some for yourself and your son. For thus says the LORD God of Israel: 'The bin of flour shall not be used up, nor shall the jar of oil run dry, until the day the LORD sends rain on the earth.'"

—1 KINGS 17:8-14

As it was in Old Testament times when the Israelites relied on God for bread and water, so it is today: we must rely on God to meet our needs.

> "For thus says the Lord God of Israel: 'The bin of flour shall not be used up, nor shall the jar of oil run dry, until the day the Lord sends rain on the earth.'"
>
> —1 Kings 17:14

MIRACLE PASSAGE

MIRACULOUS PROVISION

MIRACLE STORY

When today's miracle story begins, the prophet Elijah finds himself in the middle of a severe drought. God had been providing water for him through the brook Kerith, but after a while the brook dried up because there had been no rain. Then the word of the Lord came and directed him to make his way to the city of Zarephath. There he would meet a widow, whom God would use to provide for him.

Walking with God takes faith. As it was in Old Testament times when the Israelites relied on God for bread and water, so it is today when the world is looking everywhere for love and acceptance: we must rely on God to meet our needs.

This story of Elijah and the widow is such a powerful example of God's provision. The widow whom God said would provide for Elijah was desperate. She was preparing her last meal and had no idea God was getting ready to perform a miracle. God was testing her faith too. When the prophet requested that she bring him a cup of water and a morsel of bread, he was asking her to give him all she had.

The widow told Elijah her situation. She had no bread but only some meal, which she would mix with oil to make a last meal for herself and her son. In this response, we see her obvious respect for the prophet of God, and God saw her heart. Elijah told her, "Do not fear, for the Lord, the God of Israel,

126

will not let the jar of oil run dry until the drought ends." The widow trusted in God and therefore trusted the prophet of God. And the Lord was true to His word.

God will provide for you, just as He did for the widow at Zarephath. He will protect you.

Often it is in our times of crisis and need that we see our miracles manifest.

Can you imagine going from hopelessness to favor, from thinking you were about to have your last supper to having a source of provision that would not run dry? Had the widow not had a need in her life, she may never have seen such a dramatic miracle. God wanted to show her His power, and He wants to do the miraculous in your life too.

> Often it is in our times of crisis and need that we see our miracles manifest.

FASTING FOR CONSECRATION

FASTING PASSAGE

Put on sackcloth and lament, O priests; wail, ministers of the altar. Come, spend the night in sackcloth, ministers of my God, because the grain offering and the drink offering are withheld from the house of your God. Consecrate a fast, call a sacred assembly, assemble the elders and all the inhabitants of the land to the house of the LORD your God, and cry out to the LORD.
—JOEL 1:13–14, MEV

FASTING LESSON

When today's fasting passage begins, God's judgment is upon Judah. They had become drunkards and were disobedient to God's Law. The people had fallen away from truth and righteousness. The word of the Lord came to the prophet Joel, and he called the people to consecrate themselves—to fast and pray.

God will not be mocked. There are times in life when we become so self-sufficient that we don't recognize our need for God. When that happens, we can find ourselves turning to gods of our own making.

Joel reminded the people that their storehouses were in shambles, their barns were broken down, and their grain was ruined. Things were a mess.

Coming together in a sacred assembly and fasting was the only way the Israelites would see the truth and repent.

The word *consecrate* means to set apart for a holy purpose. This is an intentional act, time taken to reflect and rely solely on God. Over this twenty-one-day fast, you are being asked to consecrate yourself, to set yourself aside for a specific, holy purpose, to focus on truth and righteousness and ask God for insight and wisdom.

We are fasting for miracles. We are fasting to see the hand of God move. We are fasting for faith and breakthrough in our lives. As we reflect on today's fasting passage, let me ask you: Are there areas of your life that need to be repaired? Are there areas of your life that need to be surrendered to God?

Take a moment now and intentionally consecrate your heart. Offer it to God afresh and anew today.

REFLECTION TIME

In today's miracle story, we read about a widow who had lost hope for her tomorrow. The drought and famine in the land were all she could see—that is, until God showed up and provided for her need. Part of our twenty-one-day fast is to press into the supernatural realm of God and see Him do more in our lives. What action can you take to see God move in power—maybe exercise your faith, believe in your heart, or remove any room for doubt? Take a moment and write your confession to God.

_____

_____

_____

Now pray out loud for God to do what we read in Ephesians 3:20: "exceedingly abundantly above all that we ask or think." Did you notice how the widow gave all she had to the prophet of God before He did anything supernatural for her? It may have been out of fear or respect, but she gave nonetheless. Part of a righteous heart is a giving soul. Has your fast shown you anything about yourself? Miracles come from the heart of God and are released to His children. Take a moment today and intentionally do something for someone else. Taking our eyes off ourselves often leads us to see those in need. Who can you help today?

_____

_____

_____

_____

During Joel's day, ungodliness had fallen on the people
of God. They had left their first love. I think we are seeing
similar things in our world today. Lawlessness and greed
are on the rise. Joel called for the people to consecrate
themselves unto God—simply put, to set themselves apart
for a holy purpose. Today is a perfect day to consecrate
yourself—to set aside time for God alone and reflect on
His glory and majesty. Take three to five minutes right now
and offer yourself unto God afresh and anew. What would
you like to say to God right now?

_____

_____

_____

_____

_____

_____

_____

CLOSING PRAYER

Dear Lord, today I consecrate myself to You alone. I set aside anything I have placed before You. To You alone belong the glory and power and majesty. To You alone I give praise. I take myself off the altar of this world and give my whole heart to You. In Jesus' name, amen.

JOURNAL ENTRY

_____

_____

_____

_____

_____

_____

_____

_____

_____

_____

day 09

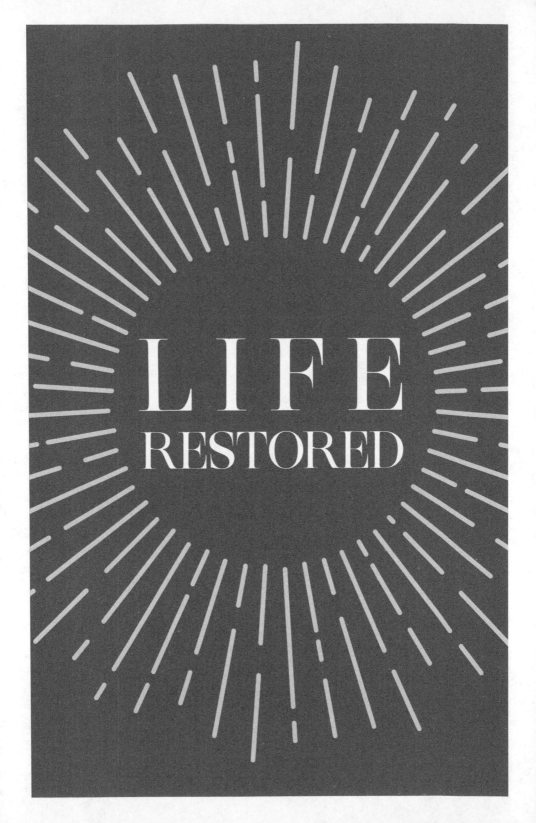

TODAY WE FIND ourselves again looking at a miracle God worked through the prophet Elijah. God didn't just restore hope—He raised a widow's son from the dead.

SCRIPTURE READING

Later on, the son of the woman, the mistress of the house, became terribly sick, so much so that he had no breath left in him. She said to Elijah, "What do I have to do with you, O you man of God? Have you come to remind me of my sin and to kill my son?"

And he said to her, "Give me your son," and he took him out of her arms and carried him up to a loft where he slept and laid him on his own bed. He cried to the LORD and said, "O LORD, my God, have You brought tragedy upon the widow with whom I live by killing her son?" And he stretched himself upon the child three times and cried to the LORD and said, "O LORD, my God, I pray that You let this child's soul come into him again."

The LORD heard the voice of Elijah, and the soul of the child came into him again, and he was revived. Elijah took the child and brought him down out of the chamber into the house and returned him to his mother, and Elijah said, "See, your son lives!"

The woman said to Elijah, "Now, because of this, I know that you are a man of God, and that the word of the LORD in your mouth is truth!"

—1 KINGS 17:17–24, MEV

The truth is that God uses all things in our lives to show us His grace and goodness. Sometimes that includes hardship.

> And he stretched himself upon the child three times and cried to the Lᴏʀᴅ and said, "O Lᴏʀᴅ, my God, I pray that You let this child's soul come into him again." The Lᴏʀᴅ heard the voice of Elijah, and the soul of the child came into him again, and he was revived.
>
> —1 Kɪɴɢs 17:21–22, ᴍᴇᴠ

MIRACLE PASSAGE

A SON IS REVIVED

As if the widow's crisis for food was not enough, now her only son lay breathless in her arms. Pouring her heart out to the prophet, the widow cried, "What more must I do for you?" Elijah took the boy in his arms, carried him to an upper room, and cried out to the Lord three times: "O Lord, my God, I pray that You let this child's soul come into him again" (v. 21). The Lord heard the voice of Elijah, and the soul of the child came back to him—he was revived.

Not only did the widow experience the miracle of the flour and oil never running out, but now her son's life had been restored!

I've often asked myself, "Would I be willing to go through this type of crisis to see God work a miracle in my life?"

I think we are so self-sufficient in our Christianity today that we talk ourselves out of miracles. We have not been encouraged to exercise our faith or expect a miracle. We simply choose to accept the hand we were dealt and live with uncomfortable circumstances.

But what if God wants more for us? What if God truly did have a plan for your crisis or your setback? What if it was the very tool God was using to do something miraculous in your life? That's a hard concept for many of us to wrap our heads around. Why would a good God ever allow crisis in our lives? Does He do it just to toy with us? Isn't that simply unkind?

I think those are important questions to ask. But if you're being honest with yourself, what would

140

God need to do to get your attention? Would you cry out to God if you didn't have a need? Are you disciplined enough to talk and walk with God daily? Would you experience intimacy and growth in your spiritual life if everything was going your way? These are questions we need to ask ourselves. These are things we need to consider. The truth is that God uses all things in our lives to show us His grace and goodness. Sometimes that includes hardship.

> I think we are so self-sufficient in our Christianity today that we talk ourselves out of miracles.

FASTING FOCUS

FASTING FOR REPENTANCE

FASTING PASSAGE

Then I set my face toward the Lord God to make request by prayer and supplications, with fasting, sackcloth, and ashes. And I prayed to the LORD my God, and made confession, and said, "O Lord, great and awesome God, who keeps His covenant and mercy with those who love Him, and with those who keep His commandments, we have sinned and committed iniquity, we have done wickedly and rebelled, even by departing from Your precepts and Your judgments. Neither have we heeded Your servants the prophets, who spoke in Your name to our kings and our princes, to our fathers and all the people of the land. O Lord, righteousness belongs to You, but to us shame of face, as it is this day—to the men of Judah, to the inhabitants of Jerusalem and all Israel, those near and those far off in all the countries to which You have driven them, because of the unfaithfulness which they have committed against You....

"O Lord, according to all Your righteousness, I pray, let Your anger and Your fury be turned away from Your city Jerusalem, Your holy mountain; because for our sins, and for the iniquities of our fathers, Jerusalem and Your people are a reproach to all those around us. Now therefore, our God, hear the prayer of Your servant, and his supplications, and for the Lord's sake cause Your face to shine on Your sanctuary, which is desolate. O my God, incline Your ear and hear; open Your eyes and see our desolations, and the city which is called by Your name; for we do not present our supplications before You because of our righteous deeds, but because of Your great mercies. O Lord, hear! O Lord, forgive! O Lord, listen and act! Do not delay for Your own sake, my God, for Your city and Your people are called by Your name."

—DANIEL 9:3–7, 16–19

FASTING LESSON

Wow! The prophet is crying out to God because of the disobedience of the people. Their hearts had grown cold to the ways of God; they were arrogant and proud. They had not listened to sound advice or heeded the Word of God. Daniel went to God in prayer, brokenness, and fasting, saying, "O God, hear my plea." Daniel knew all he could do was repent for the people's ungodliness. This is the heart of a true spiritual leader—he goes before God on behalf of others.

I for one have been saddened by the attitude and behavior of many Christians recently. The COVID-19 pandemic brought a spirit of fear, dissension, and confusion. Believers in Christ seemed to cower and hide from the world. Very few churches and faith leaders stood up to the voices of fear and control. I believe Daniel's word choice regarding ancient Israel applies to many in the church today. To us belong "shame of face" (v. 7). I believe we as the church today have been too weak to declare our testimony. I'm sure I am pushing some buttons right now, but please hear me out. Are we so different from our Old Testament family? Satan's plan is still the same: to make us fearful and too proud to ask God for help.

Daniel knew the only way to see God's blessings return to the Israelites was through confession, repentance, prayer, and *fasting*—in that order! What if we—yes, you and me and the entire body of believers—sought God with that formula and asked for forgiveness and revival in our world? Do you think we would experience something different from what we are seeing today? I do! Oh, that we might have more leaders like Daniel!

REFLECTION TIME

As if one crisis weren't enough, the widow of Zarephath faced two. The son she thought she'd lose to starvation got sick and died. Have you ever asked God *why*? Why me? Why this? Why now? How did things turn out for you? Was God with you through the storm? Did He answer your prayer or meet you in your sorrow? Did you grow through your pain? Take a minute and think through your last difficulty. Have you ever thanked God for being with you through the heartbreak? If not, thank Him now. Believe me, you will grow in your faith by trusting Him through the dark hours of the soul!

_____

_____

_____

_____

Life since the COVID pandemic has changed all of us. Many have become more fearful and reluctant to speak up for their faith. Christianity is under scrutiny and even surveillance. We read in today's passage that Daniel was not afraid to take a stand. Are you willing to stand up for your faith and the Word of God? Make a declaration of your willingness to stand strong for your conviction. Unless we are challenged to do more, most of us never will. Write your faith declaration.

_____

_____

_____

_____

Today we are fasting for repentance—an act of agreeing
with God over our sins and shortcomings and asking His
forgiveness. To repent means to admit your action was
wrong and turn around and go the other way—to do a
one-eighty in the direction of God. Unless you are perfect,
you, my friend, probably have something you can repent
for: anger, lying, betrayal, pride, fear, and so on. Take a
moment and clean the slate. Start fresh with God. Bring a
clean heart before the Lord. What do you need to repent
for?

_____

_____

_____

_____

_____

_____

_____

_____

CLOSING PRAYER

Dear Lord, today was a day of enlightenment and understanding. I want to stand strong in my conviction and be a person of character and leadership. Teach me how to speak up for what is right and not cower before those who try to intimidate me. Make me bold for Your kingdom. In Jesus' name, amen.

JOURNAL ENTRY

_____

_____

_____

_____

_____

_____

_____

_____

_____

_____

day 10

The
HEAVENS
OPEN UP

CAN YOU IMAGINE how it must have felt when the first drops of rain began to fall after three years of drought? If you've ever gone through a dry season in your life—or if you're in one right now—let today's miracle story serve as a reminder that droughts do end.

SCRIPTURE READING

Elijah said to Ahab, "Get up, eat and drink, for there is a sound of a heavy rainfall." So Ahab got up to eat and drink. And Elijah went up to the top of Carmel, and he threw himself down on the ground and put his face between his knees.

And he said to his servant, "Go up now, and look toward the sea." And he went up and looked and said, "There is nothing." And he said, "Go again," seven times. On the seventh time, he said, "A small cloud as small as a man's hand is rising out of the sea." And he said, "Go up and say to Ahab, 'Mount your chariot and get down, so that the rain does not stop you.'"

In the meantime, the sky turned black with clouds and wind, and there was a great rain. And Ahab rode and went to Jezreel. The hand of the LORD was on Elijah, and he girded up his loins and ran ahead of Ahab to the entrance of Jezreel.

—1 KINGS 18:41–46, MEV

God's plan is always to walk in unity with His children.

> On the seventh time, he said, "A small cloud as small as a man's hand is rising out of the sea." And he said, "Go up and say to Ahab, 'Mount your chariot and get down, so that the rain does not stop you.'" In the meantime, the sky turned black with clouds and wind, and there was a great rain. And Ahab rode and went to Jezreel. The hand of the LORD was on Elijah, and he girded up his loins and ran ahead of Ahab to the entrance of Jezreel.
>
> —1 KINGS 18:44–46, MEV

MIRACLE PASSAGE

FIRE FALLS FROM HEAVEN

To truly understand this miracle, we must go back to 1 Kings 17. Elijah prophesied to King Ahab that a drought was coming. Ahab was an ungodly king who led the nation of Israel to worship Baal. God had enough of the Israelites' pagan worship, and He brought a drought on the land for three years, hoping His people would repent. But instead of repenting, they remained fearful and spineless.

God had already performed the miracle for the widow in Zarephath. Now it was time for the people of Israel to see God's hand.

Ahab and all the children of Israel gathered on Mount Carmel along with Elijah and the prophets of Baal. Here God would prove His supremacy.

As the prophets of Baal cried out to their god, Elijah waited. God would not be mocked. The prophets of Baal chanted and called for Baal to come down, but there was no voice, no answer—no one paid attention.

Then it was Elijah's turn. He took a stone representing each tribe of Israel and made an altar to God. Then he dug a trench around the altar and told them to fill it with buckets of water. Now remember, this was during a three-year drought! Elijah knew God was testing the people. God was going to perform an incredible miracle.

Elijah called out for God to come down: "Hear me, O LORD, hear me, that this people may know that You are the LORD God, and that You have turned their hearts back to You again" (1 Kings 18:37). After Elijah prayed, the fire of the Lord fell and consumed the burnt offering and licked up the water that was in the trench.

The Bible tells us that when all the people saw the hand of God, they fell on their faces and cried out to the Lord: "The LORD, He is God! The LORD, He is God!" (1 Kings 18:39, MEV). Elijah commanded them to kill the prophets of Baal, for there is only One true God, and He alone is to be glorified.

This is where today's miracle story begins. Elijah looked right in the face of King Ahab and said, "Go now quickly; eat and drink, for I hear the sound of rain coming." But it wasn't raining yet.

Elijah then told his servant to go up and look toward the sea, for he was sure the rain was coming. Yet the servant saw nothing. Elijah said, "Look again."

"I see nothing, sir," the servant replied.

Elijah said, "Look again." After looking a seventh time, Elijah's servant said, "A small cloud as small as a man's hand is rising out of the sea" (1 Kings 18:44, MEV).

"Go quickly," Elijah said, "for the rain is coming, and God's glory will fall on the earth." This marked the end of the drought, and the children of Israel did indeed see God move.

I believe Elijah saw the rain coming by faith, and he was teaching his servant to look for the miracle. God was in the waiting. After seven times, the servant finally saw the slightest bit of hope. Once his hope was stirred, the servant had to activate his faith. Then he had to wait to see the manifestation of his faith grow into reality.

Often there is a miracle even in the waiting.

God's timing is perfect, but it is not always according to our schedule. Sometimes our miracle is to see the glory of God in the midst of our need.

FASTING AND CONFESSION

FASTING PASSAGE

Now on the twenty-fourth day of this month the children of Israel were assembled with fasting and sackcloth, and there was dirt on them. The offspring of Israel separated themselves from all the foreigners and then stood and confessed their sins and the iniquities of their fathers. They stood in their place and read from the Book of the Law of the LORD their God for a fourth of the day. And for another fourth, they confessed and worshipped the LORD their God.

—NEHEMIAH 9:1–3, MEV

FASTING LESSON

This passage in the Book of Nehemiah is so powerful. Prior to this account, we find the children of Israel reading the Book of the Law. They have come face to face with God's plan for their lives. They had walked away and rejected the very God who loved them. Now they were being enlightened by the Law.

The people assembled with fasting and repentance. They confessed their sins and the sins of their fathers. They read from the Book of the Law for six hours, and then for another six hours they fasted and worshipped the Lord their God. When they turned their attention to God, they saw themselves more clearly.

The same thing happens to us. When God gets

our attention, we can look at ourselves honestly and see our hearts. There is nothing more purifying than reading the Word of God. Line upon line, precept upon precept, God's Word shows us His plan for our lives.

We, like all humanity, go astray. We build our own altars, we plan our own way, and we become filled with pride and arrogance. Once again the goodness of God leads us to repentance. God's plan is always to walk in unity with His children. But the enemy always has another plan. We get to choose who we walk with. When we follow God's way, we will see the goodness of the Lord!

Often there is a miracle even in the waiting.

REFLECTION TIME

The children of Israel had once again followed after foreign gods. It seemed like the easy thing to do. God does not take our worship of any other god lightly. The drought was a way for the people to turn and cry out to their God. But that did not happen. It took the prophet crying out on their behalf. Have you put anything before God? If so, take a moment and replace any items on the throne of your heart with the glory and goodness of God. He wants to be *your* Lord. What has taken first place in your heart? Take a moment now to list those items.

_____

_____

_____

Often our miracle is on the way. Just as the servant had to go back seven times to look for the rain cloud, sometimes we must go back to our knees in faith, asking God to move. Have you given up on your miracle? Does it look like it is just too hard, it's been too long, and it's easier to just accept the way things are? If that is the case, may I ask you to go before the Lord one more time? Look for the rain cloud. It may be small, but I believe God is getting ready to rain blessings over you. Take a moment to recommit your faith, and ask God to stir your soul with confidence and expectation. God is working.

_____

_____

_____

_____

Reading the Word of God is powerful and cleansing. It does something in our spirit. After reading the Law of God, the children of Israel fasted and repented of their sin. As we have seen throughout this book, fasting is not done to show our works or our effort; it is to submit ourselves wholly to God and suppress our flesh so the presence and power of the Holy Spirit can be released in our lives. I would like to encourage you to meditate upon the Word of God today and just sit in His presence. Choose a scripture that is special to you and write it down.

_____

_____

_____

_____

_____

_____

_____

_____

CLOSING PRAYER

Dear Lord, thank You for the Word of God. It is life and power to my soul. Today as I fast, I ask You to renew my heart. I pray that I will walk in obedience and faith so others see the glory of Your presence in my life. In Jesus' name, amen.

JOURNAL ENTRY

_____

_____

_____

_____

_____

_____

_____

_____

_____

day
11

A
DOUBLE
PORTION

TODAY IS A transition day. Not only do we move from Elijah to Elisha, but we are going to go much deeper in our faith.

SCRIPTURE READING

Then Elijah said to him, "Stay here, please, for the LORD has sent me on to the Jordan." But he said, "As the LORD lives, and as your soul lives, I will not leave you!" So the two of them went on. And fifty men of the sons of the prophets went and stood facing them at a distance, while the two of them stood by the Jordan. Now Elijah took his mantle, rolled it up, and struck the water; and it was divided this way and that, so that the two of them crossed over on dry ground.

And so it was, when they had crossed over, that Elijah said to Elisha, "Ask! What may I do for you, before I am taken away from you?"

Elisha said, "Please let a double portion of your spirit be upon me."

So he said, "You have asked a hard thing. Nevertheless, if you see me when I am taken from you, it shall be so for you; but if not, it shall not be so."

Then it happened, as they continued on and talked, that suddenly a chariot of fire appeared with horses of fire and separated the two of them; and Elijah went up by a whirlwind into heaven.

And Elisha saw it, and he cried out, "My father, my father, the chariot of Israel and its horsemen!" So he saw him no more. And he took hold of his own clothes and tore them into two pieces. He also took up the mantle of Elijah that had fallen from him and went back and stood by the bank of the Jordan. Then he took the mantle of Elijah that had fallen from him, and struck the water, and said, "Where is the LORD God of Elijah?" And when he also had struck the water, it was divided this way and that; and Elisha crossed over.

Now when the sons of the prophets who were from Jericho saw him, they said, "The spirit of Elijah rests on Elisha." And they came to meet him and bowed to the ground before him. Then they said to him, "Look now, there are fifty strong men with your servants. Please let them go and search for your master, lest perhaps the Spirit of the LORD has taken him up and cast him upon some mountain or into some valley." And he said, "You shall not send anyone."

—2 KINGS 2:6–16

If we do not expect God to move, we will not see God act. Do you expect a miracle?

" Then he took the mantle of Elijah that had fallen from him, and struck the water, and said, "Where is the Lord God of Elijah?" And when he also had struck the water, it was divided this way and that; and Elisha crossed over.

—2 Kings 2:14 "

MIRACLE PASSAGE

PARTING THE JORDAN RIVER

If you know anything about these two prophets, you may know that Elijah was Elisha's mentor. He schooled him in faith, miracles, and obedience to God. Elisha was a quick learner and knew he could believe God for more. At the end of Elijah's life, Elisha asked him for a double portion of his anointing—a bold and audacious move, I would say. Yet God heard Elisha's request and acted on it. Elijah responded, "You have asked for a difficult thing, but if you see me when I am taken from you, it will happen to you. If not, it will not" (2 Kings 2:10, MEV).

Elisha did indeed see Elijah taken up in a whirl-wind, and upon Elijah's departing into heaven, Elisha picked up his mentor's mantle (cloak) and struck the Jordan River—parting it as Elijah had done. Elisha then knew the God of Elijah was now with him. As he walked across the Jordan on dry land, he could hear the sons of the prophets saying, "The spirit of Elijah rests on Elisha" (2 Kings 2:15, MEV). Elisha was indeed granted a double portion.

One of the greatest principles in today's passage is the fact that Elisha was bold enough to ask for a double portion. Elijah was one of the greatest prophets to ever live, and yet Elisha was bold enough to ask God for more. So often we compare ourselves with those we hold in high regard. They are more spiritual. They are more anointed. They are better equipped. But today is the day to ask for more: to reach higher, to believe bigger—to take your request, your prayer, your miracle to a new level!

One thing we have discussed in this book is that often we pray for a miracle but don't expect a miracle. Today we are moving into the realm of expectancy. If we do not expect God to move, we will not see God act. Do you expect a miracle?

Elisha asked, and then he received. The mantle of Elijah fell on him. It was God's timing. Second Thessalonians 3:3 says, "But the Lord is faithful, who will establish you and guard you from the evil one" (MEV). *Establish* means "to make firm or stable; to introduce and cause to grow and multiply."[1] God has established *you*. It's time to move forward in your faith, to walk in boldness and confidence. It's time to take every opportunity you have to declare the goodness of God. The mantle of God is on you.

I love the fact that Elijah told Elisha, "If you see me when I am taken from you, it will happen to you." Elisha had to *look for it*. He had to expect a miracle.

Elisha's first miracle was the same as Elijah's last miracle: the parting of the Jordan River and his crossing over on dry land. God was confirming His anointing by parting the waters for Elisha in the same manner He had done for Elijah. One was ending his ministry; the other was beginning his.

If you count the miracles of Elijah, you will find eight. If you count the miracles of Elisha, you will find sixteen.[2] When you combine those with the stories of prophetic words and prophecies, the number grows even larger.

Be so bold as to ask God for a double portion of His Spirit. All that you are believing God for through this fast, *double* it. If you are asking for one miracle, ask for two. If you are fasting one meal, increase it to two. Whatever prompted you to believe God for a miracle, go deeper with your request.

We are halfway through our fast. The second half of the journey will be the greatest. Let's believe God for greater things—and expect them! Let's see mountains move.

FASTING FOR A DOUBLE BLESSING

FASTING PASSAGES

But Daniel purposed in his heart that he would not defile himself with the portion of the king's food, nor with the wine which he drank. Therefore he requested of the master of the officials that he might not defile himself. Now God had brought Daniel into favor and compassion with the master of the officials. The master of the officials said to Daniel, "I fear my lord the king who has appointed your food and your drink. For why should he see your faces worse-looking than the youths who are your age? Then you would endanger my head before the king."

Then Daniel said to the steward, whom the master of the officials had set over Daniel, Hananiah, Mishael, and Azariah, "Please test your servants for ten days, and let them give us vegetables to eat and water to drink. Then let our countenances be looked upon before you, and the countenance of the youths who eat of the portion of the king's food. And as you see, deal with your servants." So he consented to them in this matter and tested them for ten days.

At the end of ten days their countenances appeared fairer and fatter than all the youths who ate the portion of the king's food. Thus the guard continued to take away the portion of their food and the wine that they were to drink, and gave them vegetables. As for these four youths, God gave them knowledge and skill in every branch of learning and wisdom. And Daniel had understanding in all kinds of visions and dreams.

—DANIEL 1:8–17, MEV

In those days I, Daniel, was mourning three full weeks. I ate no pleasant food, no meat or wine came into my mouth, nor did I anoint myself at all, till three whole weeks were fulfilled.

—DANIEL 10:2–3

FASTING LESSON

Today's fasting passages are where we find the Daniel fast. The story of Daniel is one we all admire. He was a strong, good-looking, confident, capable young man who was taken captive and brought into a foreign land to serve a king named Nebuchadnezzar. Yet his faith and resolve were evident.

The king thought it was kind to share his wine and pleasant foods with a foreign young man in his court. However, Daniel sought to please his God. He asked the king to test him and his friends, who were also Israelites in captivity. For ten days they would eat no pleasant foods nor drink any wine; they would consume only water and vegetables. At the end of the ten days they would see who the healthier men were. Daniel chose to fast from those items to show the power of his God. The Bible tells us that at the end of the ten days, the children of Israel looked stronger and healthier than the king's men.

This Daniel fast is one many people choose today. Abstaining from wine, animal products, and preservatives is a demonstration of faith and expectancy. Whichever fast you have chosen for these twenty-one days, it is your offering to God. Daniel was given favor, and God promoted him to positions of leadership. Ask God today to anoint you with favor and power. Be firm in your conviction. Make bold requests and stand strong in your foundation.

REFLECTION TIME

Can you say, "More power"? Both in our miracle story and our fasting passage, we read about two people who were not afraid to trust God for more. What would a double portion look like for you?

_____

_____

_____

Today we reflected on the definition of the word *establish*. Again, 2 Thessalonians 3:3 says, "The Lord is faithful, who will establish you and guard you from the evil one" (MEV). *Establish* means "to make firm or stable; to introduce and cause to grow and multiply."[3] God wants *you* to grow and multiply. In what way would you like to see God multiply your life? What would spiritual growth look like for you?

_____

_____

_____

Daniel was not intimidated by the king's men but instead asked permission to abstain from certain foods and fast for ten days. As he fasted, I'm sure he prayed for God to be seen as Yahweh, the true and living God. Daniel had a mission, and it was to glorify God. How has your fast touched others' lives? We do not fast for man's approval or opinion, but in our fasting others do see the glory of God. Share your story of fasting.

_____

_____

_____

_____

_____

_____

_____

_____

_____

_____

_____

_____

_____

CLOSING PRAYER

Dear Lord, thank You for allowing me to partner with You in sharing my testimony. What You have done in my life is evidence to the world of the power of salvation. I pray that I will always lift You high and exalt Your name above all names. In Jesus' name, amen.

JOURNAL ENTRY

_____

_____

_____

_____

_____

_____

_____

_____

_____

_____

day 12

OIL
THAT
DOESN'T
RUN OUT

WE KNOW ELISHA received a double portion of the anointing on Elijah's life, and today we'll look at a miracle that is similar to one that happened in Elijah's life—when a widow's oil did not run out.

SCRIPTURE READING

A certain woman of the wives of the sons of the prophets cried out to Elisha, saying, "Your servant my husband is dead, and you know that your servant feared the LORD. And the creditor is coming to take my two sons to be his slaves."

So Elisha said to her, "What shall I do for you? Tell me, what do you have in the house?" And she said, "Your maidservant has nothing in the house but a jar of oil."

Then he said, "Go, borrow vessels from everywhere, from all your neighbors—empty vessels; do not gather just a few. And when you have come in, you shall shut the door behind you and your sons; then pour it into all those vessels, and set aside the full ones."

So she went from him and shut the door behind her and her sons, who brought the vessels to her; and she poured it out. Now it came to pass, when the vessels were full, that she said to her son, "Bring me another vessel."

And he said to her, "There is not another vessel." So the oil ceased. Then she came and told the man of God. And he said, "Go, sell the oil and pay your debt; and you and your sons live on the rest."

—2 KINGS 4:1–7

Remember,
God will not
be mocked. He
knows all and
sees all. He's
a good and
righteous judge—
and His truth
will always be
revealed.

> Then he said, "Go, borrow vessels from everywhere, from all your neighbors—empty vessels; do not gather just a few. And when you have come in, you shall shut the door behind you and your sons; then pour it into all those vessels and set aside the full ones."
>
> —2 Kings 4:3-4

MIRACLE PASSAGE

FULL VESSELS

What a story of faith! Today's miracle story is one that has always encouraged me. Here we have a woman whose husband was dead. He was one of the servants of Elisha and clearly a man of God. Now he was gone, and his wife was desperate. She had no food, no money, and no resources; she had only two sons who were about to be taken as slaves. So she cried out to the prophet Elisha, "My husband is dead, and I have nowhere to go. I need a miracle!"

"What do you have in your house?" the prophet asked.

"Just a little oil," she replied.

Elisha said, "Go and gather every vessel you can find, and do not gather just a few."

This part of the story has always intrigued me because the woman's provision to meet her need was dependent upon her response. She gathered every pot, kettle, bucket, and vessel she could find, and then, as the prophet instructed, she went inside and closed the door. And she poured. And she poured. And she poured—until all the vessels were full.

Let me stop right here and ask you how many vessels *you* would have gathered. Enough to get you through your crisis? Enough to fill the room? God wants to fill our vessels—and *we are the vessels*. God wants to continually fill us up with His oil, the oil of the Holy Spirit. But often our vessels are already full: full of works and self-righteousness, full of dreams and ideas, full of our schedules and family obligations. Often our vessels can't be filled because they are already filled with the wrong oil.

This widow was desperate, and she continued to pour until the vessels ran out. This was a miracle of God.

The woman collected enough oil to pay off her creditors. She also had enough resources for her and her boys to live out their days. In the same way, God paid off our debt through the blood of Jesus. He has poured His oil and grace on each and every one of us.

Today let's ask for a double portion. Ask for God's favor, God's goodness, God's increase, and God's reward. Let your vessel be filled with the Holy Spirit of God.

> Today let's ask for a double portion. Ask for God's favor, God's goodness, God's increase, and God's reward.

FASTING FOR GOOD CHOICES

FASTING PASSAGE

So Ahab said to Elijah, "Have you found me, O my enemy?" And he answered, "I have found you, because you have sold yourself to do evil in the sight of the LORD: 'Behold, I will bring calamity on you. I will take away your posterity, and will cut off from Ahab every male in Israel, both bond and free. I will make your house like the house of Jeroboam the son of Nebat, and like the house of Baasha the son of Ahijah, because of the provocation with which you have provoked Me to anger, and made Israel sin.' And concerning Jezebel the Lord also spoke, saying, 'The dogs shall eat Jezebel by the wall of Jezreel.'

"The dogs shall eat whoever belongs to Ahab and dies in the city, and the birds of the air shall eat whoever dies in the field." But there was no one like Ahab who sold himself to do wickedness in the sight of the LORD, because Jezebel his wife stirred him up. And he behaved very abominably in following idols, according to all *that* the Amorites had done, whom the LORD had cast out before the children of Israel. So it was, when Ahab heard those words, that he tore his clothes and put sackcloth on his body, and fasted and lay in sackcloth, and went about mourning. And the word of the LORD came to Elijah the Tishbite, saying, "See how Ahab has humbled himself before Me? Because he has humbled himself before Me, I will not bring the calamity in his days. In the days of his son I will bring the calamity on his house."

—1 KINGS 21:20–29

FASTING LESSON

Today's fasting passage is one of the most intriguing stories in the Bible. It tells us that King Ahab tore his clothes, fasted, and went about mourning because of the Lord's words to him. But first you must know the context of the story.

The king was married to a wicked and cruel woman named Jezebel. She spared no expense to do evil and harm against God's children. She worshipped the god of Baal and did all she could to convince the king to join her in her rituals.

The story in 1 Kings 21 is about a certain man who had a vineyard King Ahab wanted. Ahab was sad and sullen because the man would not sell him the vineyard.

Ahab's wife, Jezebel, took matters into her own hands. Jezebel set the stage for the landowner to be falsely accused, and he was stoned to death and his property given to the king. When the prophet Elisha heard about the wickedness of Ahab and Jezebel, he brought a prophetic word of judgment and death upon them. King Ahab was remorseful and sought God with prayer and fasting.

The passage tells us that God received his prayer and confession—but he never lived a life with God's blessing and anointing. God does see our fast, and He knows our repentance. But our actions and choices matter. Ahab was a wicked man who allowed himself to be influenced by an even more wicked woman. Remember, God will not be mocked. He knows all and sees all. He's a good and righteous judge—and His truth will always be revealed.

REFLECTION TIME

I can only imagine the heartbreak and despair of the widow in today's miracle story. She had no husband and no money, and her only sons were about to be taken away. She needed a miracle. She cried out to God, and her prayer was heard. But then her faith was tested. How far would you go if you were given the word that was given to her: "Go get vessels to fill up with the few ounces of oil you currently have"? She poured in faith. The oil did not run out. Her faith did not run out. Only the vessels ran out. Today, ask God to increase your faith. Ask Him to cause it to grow and expand so you can see the hand of God in your life. In what areas do you need your faith to grow?

_____

_____

_____

_____

We have talked a lot about the reason we fast. It's not for show; we fast as an act of faith and surrender. Again, fasting tempers our flesh and activates our spirit. Like King Ahab, we must all repent for our past choices and seek the face of God. We all want our miracle to happen, but our heart may not be in the right place to see God move. Take a moment now and reexamine your motive for fasting. Write what you want to see from this time of examination.

_____

_____

_____

_____

King Ahab was influenced by his evil wife. He did not have the courage to stand up to her wicked plans but instead sulked like a child. There have been times in all our lives when we did not stand up for what we knew to be right. Take a moment now and think of ways you can speak up for your convictions. How can you stand up for your faith?

_____

_____

_____

_____

_____

_____

_____

_____

_____

_____

_____

CLOSING PRAYER

Dear Lord, I have not always been bold with my testimony. I ask that You forgive my timidity and create a strong and steadfast spirit within me. I desire to be a leader for the cause of Christ. Fill me with Your Spirit and increase my faith. In Jesus' name, amen.

JOURNAL ENTRY

day 13

TAKE the PLUNGE

MANY OF US have needed God to bring miraculous healing. Today we will look at the unique way God healed Naaman of leprosy and what the Holy Spirit may want us to learn from his experience.

SCRIPTURE READING

Now Naaman, commander of the army of the king of Syria, was a great and honorable man in the eyes of his master, because by him the Lord had given victory to Syria. He was also a mighty man of valor, but a leper. And the Syrians had gone out on raids and had brought back captive a young girl from the land of Israel. She waited on Naaman's wife. Then she said to her mistress, "If only my master were with the prophet who is in Samaria! For he would heal him of his leprosy." And Naaman went in and told his master, saying, "Thus and thus said the girl who is from the land of Israel."

Then the king of Syria said, "Go now, and I will send a letter to the king of Israel."

So he departed and took with him ten talents of silver, six thousand shekels of gold, and ten changes of clothing. Then he brought the letter to the king of Israel, which said, Now be advised, when this letter comes to you, that I have sent Naaman my servant to you, that you may heal him of his leprosy.

And it happened, when the king of Israel read the letter, that he tore his clothes and said, "Am I God, to kill and make alive, that this man sends a man to me to heal him of his leprosy? Therefore please consider, and see how he seeks a quarrel with me."

So it was, when Elisha the man of God heard that the king of Israel had torn his clothes, that he sent to the king, saying, "Why have you torn your clothes? Please let him come to me, and he shall know that there is a prophet in Israel."

Then Naaman went with his horses and chariot, and he stood at the door of Elisha's house. And Elisha sent a messenger to him, saying, "Go and wash in the Jordan seven times, and your flesh shall be restored to you, and you shall be clean."

But Naaman became furious, and went away and said, "Indeed, I said to myself, 'He will surely come out to me, and stand and call on the name of the Lord his God, and wave his hand over the place, and heal the leprosy.' Are not the Abanah and the Pharpar, the rivers of Damascus, better than all the waters of Israel? Could I not wash in them and be clean?" So he turned and went away in a rage.

And his servants came near and spoke to him, and said, "My father, if the prophet had told you to do something great, would you not have done it? How much more then, when he says to you, 'Wash, and be clean'?" So he went down and dipped seven times in the Jordan, according to the saying of the man of God; and his flesh was restored like the flesh of a little child, and he was clean.

—2 KINGS 5:1–14

> "So he went down and dipped seven times in the Jordan, according to the saying of the man of God; and his flesh was restored like the flesh of a little child, and he was clean.
>
> —2 Kings 5:14

MIRACLE PASSAGE

LEPROSY HEALED

Money can buy a lot of things, but it cannot buy your health. Naaman was a man with leprosy. Being a soldier, he could hide his skin by wearing his uniform. But when he came home at night, it was the same story—he was a leper. The young housemaid who served his family was a follower of God. She had heard the miracle stories of the prophet Elisha and said to her mistress, "If only my master could make his way to the prophet Elisha, he could be healed of leprosy."

Against all odds, Naaman asked the king of Syria if he could go see the prophet. The king of Syria took it upon himself to write a letter to the king of Israel, asking for Naaman's healing. The problem was, he was asking the wrong king. The king of Israel replied, "I have no power to heal your servant."

Yet hearing of Naaman's appeal to the king of Israel, Elisha asked for Naaman to be sent to him.

Naaman approached Elisha's house feeling hopeful. Now remember, God does not always answer our prayers in the way we think. The man of God sent his servant to the door to tell Naaman how to be healed of his leprosy: "Go and wash yourself seven times in the Jordan River."

"What?" Naaman said. "I am a man held in high regard, and I expect to be treated with respect! Me, dip in the dirty Jordan? Are you crazy? Forget this." He probably thought, "I knew this was too good to be true."

But his servants grabbed him and said, "Sir, if the prophet had told you to do something more difficult, would you not have done it? It's simple; just go dip seven times in the Jordan River."

Following Elisha's instructions required faith. Once again we find in this story that God often will ask us to do things to stretch our faith—to teach us to trust Him.

Naaman knew he had no other option. He went to the Jordan and dipped once, twice, three times, and with no results. He dipped four, five, six times, and still nothing. "This seems far-fetched," he probably thought, "but I will go down one more time." Naaman dipped a seventh time by faith in the Jordan River—and he came up whole. His skin was like that of a newborn baby.

I think God likes the number seven, for it was on the seventh day that He rested. And now for the first time, Naaman could understand rest—resting as a new creation by faith. He was healed through the hand of the prophet and the heart of a good God. Are you willing to take the plunge? Will you trust God's ways even if they don't make sense to you? Will you allow Him to stretch your faith so you can grow in your trust and confidence in Him? Just as it was with Naaman, walking by faith requires action on our part.

> # Fasting is a way to measure and consider the intentions of our hearts.

FASTING FOR REVELATION

FASTING PASSAGE

In the fourth year of Jehoiakim the son of Josiah, king of Judah, this word came to Jeremiah from the LORD, saying: Take a scroll of a book, and write in it all the words that I have spoken to you against Israel and against Judah and against all the nations, from the day I spoke to you, from the days of Josiah, even to this day. It may be that the house of Judah will hear all the disaster which I intend to do to them, so that every man may turn from his evil way; then I will forgive their iniquity and their sin....

In the fifth year of Jehoiakim the son of Josiah, king of Judah, in the ninth month, they proclaimed a fast before the LORD to all the people in Jerusalem and to all the people who came from the cities of Judah to Jerusalem. Then Baruch read from the book the words of Jeremiah in the house of the LORD, in the chamber of Gemariah the son of Shaphan the scribe, in the higher court, at the entry of the New Gate of the house of the LORD, in the ears of all the people.

—JEREMIAH 36:1–3, 9–10, MEV

FASTING LESSON

Have you ever read the Old Testament and wondered why God seems so angry? Well, in truth, He is not angry—He is loving. He is a righteous and holy Father who desires that the hearts of His children be wholly devoted to Him. It's the people of Israel who are angry. They are the ones who walked away from God and filled their hearts with pride and entitlement. God's desire has *always* been to bring His children back to His heart.

In today's passage the children of Israel once again had walked away from God. At the beginning of the chapter God told Jeremiah to write the words of the prophecy. This was so future generations would know the story and legacy of God's love. God loves to give us prophetic words—words of promise and hope.

Even though the children of Israel were in rebellion against God, they still participated in ritual fasting. It was not until a year after Jeremiah gave the prophecy that the people proclaimed a fast before the Lord with a pure heart and asked Him to do a new work in them (v. 9).

Fasting can quickly become a ritual or religious act. That is why we must always examine our hearts and motives. A pure fast before the Lord is what God desires. One of the many things we still hold in common with our Old Testament family is that we also have hearts of entitlement and pride. Fasting is a way to measure and consider the intentions of our hearts.

REFLECTION TIME

Naaman had a hard time with the assignment the prophet Elisha gave him. "Really?" he thought. "Dip seven times in the Jordan River? Why that river? Can't the prophet find a cleaner place to perform a miracle?" Yet God had a reason. He wanted to heal more than Naaman's leprosy—He wanted to heal his heart. God sees more than we think, and He knows exactly what it will take to purify our hearts. God wants to heal you in an area you may not even know needs healing. Ask God to show you where you need healing today. You might be surprised. Now allow Him to show you the steps you must take to receive His healing. What is God showing you today?

_____

_____

_____

_____

Did you notice in today's fasting passage that God told Jeremiah to write the prophecy He was getting ready to give him? It would be for future generations to hear about the goodness of God and His plan for humanity. Writing our story is a gift we can leave to our children and grandchildren. God tells His people throughout the Scriptures to write their testimony and the precepts of the Lord. If you do not have a journal to record your journey, let me encourage you to get one today and begin to write your story. It will be one of the greatest gifts you can give to the next generation. What one thing would you like to tell someone about your spiritual journey?

_____

_____

_____

_____

In today's fasting lesson, we read that the children of God continued their fasting tradition even in the midst of their rebellion and disobedience. Fasting for them was routine, a practice that was part of their religious culture. But God was not impressed. It was not until they came to God with a pure heart that He heard their request and healed the people. Why do you think it is so easy for us to go back to our old way of life—our bad behavior and self-indulgent lifestyles? Do you find yourself going back and forth in your walk with God? What is the trigger that trips you up? Have a dialogue with God about this. What do you need to say to Him?

_____

_____

_____

_____

_____

_____

CLOSING PRAYER

Dear Lord, I desire for my testimony to be heard. I ask that You give me the words to speak out for You today. I desire to go deeper in my understanding of Your love and goodness. Show me how to hear Your voice. My heart is to seek Your kingdom above all others. I want You to be first in my life. In Jesus' name, amen.

JOURNAL ENTRY

_____

_____

_____

_____

_____

_____

_____

_____

_____

day
14

OPEN
EYES

Have you ever felt overwhelmed by a situation you were facing, something you thought you just couldn't see a way out of? Elisha's servant could probably relate to that feeling. The miracle God performed didn't just change the situation he found himself in but also his perspective when the Lord opened his eyes to see what was happening in the spirit realm.

SCRIPTURE READING

Therefore the heart of the king of Syria was greatly troubled by this thing; and he called his servants and said to them, "Will you not show me which of us is for the king of Israel?"

And one of his servants said, "None, my lord, O king; but Elisha, the prophet who is in Israel, tells the king of Israel the words that you speak in your bedroom."

So he said, "Go and see where he is, that I may send and get him."

And it was told him, saying, "Surely he is in Dothan."

Therefore he sent horses and chariots and a great army there, and they came by night and surrounded the city. And when the servant of the man of God arose early and went out, there was an army, surrounding the city with horses and chariots. And his servant said to him, "Alas, my master! What shall we do?"

So he answered, "Do not fear, for those who are with us are more than those who are with them." And Elisha prayed, and said, "Lord, I pray, open his eyes that he may see." Then the Lord opened the eyes of the young man, and he saw. And behold, the mountain was full of horses and chariots of fire all around Elisha. So when the Syrians came down to him, Elisha prayed to the Lord, and said, "Strike this people, I pray, with blindness." And He struck them with blindness according to the word of Elisha.

Now Elisha said to them, "This is not the way, nor is this the city. Follow me, and I will bring you to the man whom you seek." But he led them to Samaria. So it was, when they had come to Samaria, that Elisha said, "Lord, open the eyes of these men, that they may see." And the Lord opened their eyes, and they saw; and there they were, inside Samaria!

—2 Kings 6:11–20

> And Elisha prayed, and said, "LORD, I pray, open his eyes that he may see." Then the LORD opened the eyes of the young man, and he saw. And behold, the mountain was full of horses and chariots of fire all around Elisha.
>
> —2 KINGS 6:17

MIRACLE PASSAGE

ARMIES OF ANGELS

You are never alone. God is with you, and He is for you. If you are a believer in Jesus Christ, God is in you. And you also are surrounded by an army of angels. Hebrews 12:1 instructs, "Therefore we also, since we are surrounded by so great a cloud of witnesses, let us lay aside every weight, and the sin which so easily ensnares us, and let us run with endurance the race that is set before us."

Elisha had seen God perform many miracles. There had been good times and bad times, lean times and prosperous times. But they all pointed him to the one true God and King, who gives life and breath. In this story Elisha once again found himself in the midst of a battle. His enemies had come to encircle him, to bring war and take his life. Yet the prophet was able to rest in the confidence that God had his back.

His servant, not so much.

All the servant could see was the city surrounded by their adversary. "How can you rest at a time like this, for we are going to be killed," he wondered. So the prophet of God, the man of faith, the man's mentor and father figure, cried out, "O Lord, open his eyes so he might see." Immediately, the servant saw that the mountains were full of horses and chariots of fire all around Elisha.

With his next breath Elisha prayed, "O God, close the eyes of our enemy with blindness." And God struck the enemy army with blindness, according to the word of Elisha. With confidence and assurance, Elisha led the enemy army right into the hands of the king of Israel.

Have you ever had one of those moments when, out of the blue, you knew you were protected and God was with you? Have you stopped to consider that moments like those aren't extraordinary but everyday occurrences that you're just not always aware of? Have you considered that every single day God is protecting you with His army of angels? In the supernatural realm, there are always those fighting on our behalf, defending us from evil. Don't ever forget the response of the prophet Elisha in verse 16: "Do not fear, for those who are with us are more than those who are with them." The Bible says, "Greater is he that is in you, than he that is in the world" (1 John 4:4, KJV). God has come to give you life and life more abundantly (John 10:10).

God always has a plan. He has a miracle in the works. The question is, What do you see—what the enemy is doing or what God is doing?

Ask God to open your eyes in the middle of your affliction, temptation, trial, or grief. Ask Him to open the eyes of your heart and give you insight, wisdom, and revelation.

FASTING TO EXPRESS GRIEF

FASTING FOCUS

FASTING PASSAGE

Then David took hold of his clothes and tore them, as did all of the men who were with him. They mourned and wept and fasted until evening for Saul, Jonathan his son, the people of the LORD, and the house of Israel, because they had fallen by the sword.

—2 SAMUEL 1:11–12, MEV

FASTING LESSON

The death of a loved one is devastating—especially when the person's life has been taken from him. David and Jonathan had a special bond, a true friendship. Even though Jonathan's father, King Saul, despised David, the two young men had a kindred friendship.

Today's fasting passage tells us that David mourned and wept and fasted for Saul and Jonathan. Saul was still the king, and David understood authority. He knew he was next in line to be king, but he would be crowned in God's timing, which is always perfect, even when we're in the midst of sorrow. David had to say goodbye to his best friend, Jonathan, while being ready to step into leadership as the next king.

The Bible tells us that David and his men mourned, wept, and fasted. Once again, we see fasting as a means to bring our hearts before God.

It is an opportunity for us to sit in silence and contemplation and allow God to do His perfect work in our lives. Saul's death marked the close of a chapter in David's life. David took the time he needed to finish the season well, because in his next act he would be king.

This would not be the last time David would fast to heal a broken heart. It would, however, set the stage for understanding the purpose and power of coming to God with a pure heart and a contrite spirit. As a man willing to fast and seek God for comfort after the death of his friend, David was on a journey of knowing God in a much deeper way.

> # Once again, we see fasting as a means to bring our hearts before God.

REFLECTION TIME

Have you had days when all you could see were defeat and discouragement? Have you had days when it seemed like your trouble was bigger than your solution? Well then, you are in good company. From our miracle story today, we see that God always has an army of angels ready and waiting to meet our needs. Take a moment right now to thank God for His constant watchcare and presence. How do you need God to show up for you today?

_____

_____

_____

_____

In 2 Samuel 1, David was mourning the loss of his best friend. He and Jonathan had shared many experiences. Now Jonathan was gone. Fasting is a natural part of brokenness, but I believe David's fast was more than that. I believe David was fasting to seek comfort after the loss of his friend. David knew only God could bring the hope and consolation he needed. Have you ever had a broken heart and just needed the love of God to comfort you? Share your thoughts and memories. God will meet you in your moment.

_____

_____

_____

_____

David knew he would be the next king of Israel, but he was patient in the process. His friend Jonathan's father was king, and David had respect and honor for the role. But now it was his turn to rule and lead the people. He had already been anointed as the next king of Israel. After grieving the loss of his friend, David was ready to step into his assignment. Have you ever lost someone and just felt crippled by the experience? God has assignments for us all. Take some time and think about how God might be preparing you for a new assignment. What is God saying to you now?

_____

_____

_____

_____

_____

_____

_____

_____

_____

_____

_____

CLOSING PRAYER

Dear Lord, I know You have new assignments for me. I trust Your perfect plan and Your calling on my life. Show me how to step out in faith and lead others as You have gifted me to do. I give You my heartache and grief and ask You to comfort me with Your love and empower me with Your Spirit. In Jesus' name, amen.

JOURNAL ENTRY

_____

_____

_____

_____

_____

_____

_____

_____

_____

MIRACLES in the LIVES of JESUS and HIS DISCIPLES

TODAY WE START WEEK 3 of our fast. It's time to transition into the New Testament, into the lives of Jesus and the disciples. As we will see, miracles happened in the New Testament as well as the Old. From creation to the resurrection of Jesus, miracles are part of our faith. There are eighty miracles[1] recorded in the New Testament, but for our time together we will be looking at only seven.

day
15

WATER INTO WINE

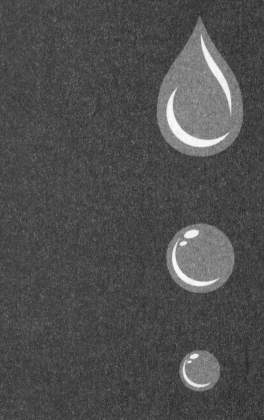

IT COULD BE argued that today's miracle wasn't even supposed to happen. Jesus said it wasn't time for Him to reveal Himself, but His mother asked Him for a favor, and Jesus responded to her request and turned water into wine. In some ways the issue was minor. Running out of wine wouldn't have been the end of the world. But isn't it great to know God cares even about the small things? Be encouraged today that none of your requests are insignificant to Him.

SCRIPTURE READING

On the third day there was a wedding in Cana of Galilee. The mother of Jesus was there. Both Jesus and His disciples were invited to the wedding. When the wine ran out, the mother of Jesus said to Him, "They have no wine." Jesus said to her, "Woman, what does this have to do with Me? My hour has not yet come."

His mother said to the servants, "Whatever He says to you, do it." Six water pots made of stone were sitting there, used for ceremonial cleansing by the Jews, containing twenty to thirty gallons each. Jesus said to them, "Fill the water pots with water." And they filled them up to the brim. Then He said to them, "Now draw some out, and take it to the master of the feast."

And they took it. When the master of the feast tasted the water that had been turned into wine, and did not know where it came from (though the servants who drew the water knew), the master of the feast called the bridegroom, and he said to him, "Every man serves the good wine first, and after men have drunk freely, then the poor wine is served. But you have kept the good wine until now."

This, the first of His signs, Jesus did in Cana of Galilee, and He revealed His glory, and His disciples believed in Him.

—JOHN 2:1-11, MEV

"

Jesus said to them, "Fill the water pots with water." And they filled them up to the brim. Then He said to them, "Now draw some out, and take it to the master of the feast." And they took it. When the master of the feast tasted the water that had been turned into wine, and did not know where it came from (though the servants who drew the water knew), the master of the feast called the bridegroom, and he said to him, "Every man serves the good wine first, and after men have drunk freely, then the poor wine is served. But you have kept the good wine until now."

—JOHN 2:7–10, MEV

"

MIRACLE PASSAGE

A MIRACLE AT A WEDDING

Turning water into wine was the first miracle of Jesus. He had accompanied His mother to a wedding celebration. Some scholars think it may have been one of Mary's relatives who was getting married, so both she and Jesus would have known the guests well. By some accounts, Cana was only a short distance from Nazareth, so it was likely a town they knew well too.

Can you imagine what this might have been like for Mary, this woman who claimed to have given birth to the Son of God? As soon as she arrived, suspicion was probably growing in the minds of the villagers: "Isn't this our Mary? Mary from Nazareth—you know, Joseph's wife? I heard she had a son, and He is supposedly the Son of God. Jesus, they call Him. 'Messiah,' I heard some say."

I can only imagine the rumor mill in that little village. If Jesus truly was divine, where were the signs and wonders? When was He going to do something supernatural, something that proved His divinity? The people wouldn't have long to wait for the moment of His unveiling when He would reveal Himself through signs, wonders, and divine power.

If this wedding was like many today, it probably cost more than anyone imagined. Friends invite friends who were not expected, the food and beverage selection seem to get bigger, and the total cost of the event exceeds the budget. If this is what happened at the wedding in Cana, last-minute corners had to be cut. But the only thing worse than the bride not showing up was to run out of wine—and that is exactly what happened.

Here was Jesus at this beautiful celebration of a man and woman exchanging vows in the sacred act of marriage, and they were out of wine. After Mary enlisted His help, Jesus asked for the water pots to be brought to Him, and He turned the water into wine. But it wasn't just any wine. It was a magnificent wine, a new wine, a sommelier's dream. "Why did you save the best for last?" the guests inquired.

I can only imagine the conversation around the water well the next day. "Maybe He is the Messiah," some undoubtedly whispered. "Maybe He is the Son of God. Who knows, maybe He'll turn this well into wine next."

Some questioned the encounter. Some believed. And others held these things quietly in their hearts. This was Jesus' first recorded miracle—the divine was touching humanity.

At the wedding in Cana, the barrels had run dry. But Jesus never runs dry. He fills our soul with a new wine—the wine of the Spirit.

May I ask you, Where have you run dry? Where do you feel depleted, lonely, disappointed, overextended?

Jesus can perform a miracle in your life. He can turn your dry and thirsty soul into one that is refreshed, joyful, and expectant.

FASTING FOR PURITY

FASTING PASSAGE

Moreover, when you fast, do not be like the hypocrites with a sad countenance. For they disfigure their faces so they may appear to men to be fasting. Truly I say to you, they have their reward. But you, when you fast, anoint your head and wash your face, so that you will not appear to men to be fasting, but to your Father who is in secret. And your Father who sees in secret will reward you openly.

—Matthew 6:16–18, mev

FASTING LESSON

I love this fasting passage in Matthew. It comes right after Jesus teaches His disciples the Lord's Prayer. Matthew 6 begins with Jesus telling His disciples to guard the intentions of their hearts and not do acts of kindness for others to see their good works, but solely to please God.

When you pray, you shall not be like the hypocrites. For they love to pray standing in the synagogues and on the street corners that they may be seen by men. Truly I say to you, they have their reward.

—Matthew 6:5, mev

After He told the disciples how they should pray, He moved into today's fasting passage, again emphasizing the need to watch our motives. When we fast,

He said, we shouldn't be like the hypocrites who make a show of their fasting because they want to be seen by men.

I find it interesting that Jesus said "when you fast," not "*if* you choose to fast." This was a deep conversation Jesus was having with His disciples. They were fully aware of the discipline of fasting, for it was part of their tradition, yet they lacked power. So Jesus taught them something new. He taught them a spiritual exercise with a divine outcome—that fasting is powerful when it isn't just a good work but an act of obedience. When you fast with the right motive, "your Father who sees in secret will reward you openly," as Matthew 6:18 states.

Fasting is an act of our will, a discipline of our flesh. It teaches us not to rely on the sustenance of the world but to seek a higher satisfaction, a higher purpose.

Jesus was teaching His disciples to seek communion and a pure relationship with God. This is always His aim. Whether He's preaching about new wine or giving a new understanding of old paradigms, Jesus is always teaching us to trust Him more and go deeper in our relationship with Him.

What is He saying to you right now?

> # At the wedding in Cana, the barrels had run dry. But Jesus never runs dry.

REFLECTION TIME

In today's miracle story, we learned that Jesus cares about people. He wanted the wedding to be perfect. And in making sure the guests didn't run out of wine, He introduced Himself as the Messiah—Jesus the Miracle Worker. Jesus has a way of meeting us in our story. When was the last time you felt Jesus close to you?

_____

_____

_____

_____

I am sure many in Cana doubted Jesus was the Son of God. Those who knew Him as a young boy were suspicious of His claims. Yet no one could dismiss His miracles. Why do you think Jesus chose to turn water into wine as His first public miracle? Take a moment to reflect on this question.

_____

_____

_____

_____

Jesus uses the conclusion of the Lord's Prayer to introduce the topic of fasting to His disciples. He knew it was a tradition the Israelites observed, yet He saw that they lacked

power and faith to see their fast manifest into miracles.
Jesus thought it was the perfect time to teach them about
fasting with a right motive. Check your heart and your
reason for joining this fast experience. Reflection is always
a good thing to do with God. Share a little bit of your
fasting experience.

_____

_____

_____

_____

_____

_____

_____

_____

_____

_____

_____

_____

CLOSING PRAYER

Dear Lord, thank You for caring for me and my story. Thank You for taking the dry parts of my life and turning them into new wine. Today I recommit myself on this journey of expecting a miracle. I know with You all things are possible. In Jesus' name, amen.

JOURNAL ENTRY

_____

_____

_____

_____

_____

_____

_____

_____

_____

_____

_____

_____

day
16

RISE and WALK

SOMETIMES THE MIRACLE isn't just for our benefit. Today as we read about Jesus healing a paralyzed man, we'll see that more lives were touched than just that of the man who, for the first time in who knows how long, picked up his bed and walked home.

SCRIPTURE READING

So He got into a boat, crossed over, and came to His own city. Then behold, they brought to Him a paralytic lying on a bed. When Jesus saw their faith, He said to the paralytic, "Son, be of good cheer; your sins are forgiven you." And at once some of the scribes said within themselves, "This Man blasphemes!"

But Jesus, knowing their thoughts, said, "Why do you think evil in your hearts? For which is easier, to say, 'Your sins are forgiven you,' or to say, 'Arise and walk'? But that you may know that the Son of Man has power on earth to forgive sins"—then He said to the paralytic, "Arise, take up your bed, and go to your house." And he arose and departed to his house. Now when the multitudes saw it, they marveled and glorified God, who had given such power to men.

—MATTHEW 9:1-8

When we hear miracle stories or witness evidence of a miracle, our faith does indeed increase.

> "For which is easier, to say, 'Your sins are forgiven you,' or to say, 'Arise and walk'? But that you may know that the Son of Man has power on earth to forgive sins"— then He said to the paralytic, "Arise, take up your bed, and go to your house." And he arose and departed to his house.
>
> —MATTHEW 9: 5–7

MIRACLE PASSAGE

WHICH IS EASIER?

I love the way Jesus posed His question to the religious leaders: Which is easier to do, heal the man of his sickness or forgive his sins? The two are equal when you are the Son of God; one is not more difficult than the other. God does not expend energy to heal or forgive us because He is God. He is not bound by humanity. He is not bound by confines of energy or effort. He is limitless.

I think it's telling that the scripture says Jesus saw their faith—faith to be healed and faith to be saved. This miracle of healing was also a miracle of faith. It takes the same amount of faith to be healed as it does to be saved. Faith has only one ingredient: belief in Jesus, the Son of God, to heal, forgive, and cleanse us of our sins.

It was the miraculous healing of the paralytic that caused the people to believe. But ultimately our faith must be based on a conviction, a confidence in God's Word, and not signs and wonders.

Today people look for evidence of God through healings or spiritual acts. But the Bible tells us in Romans 10:17, "Faith comes by hearing, and hearing by the word of God" (MEV).

The purpose of this and every other miracle Jesus performed was the same: to bring glory to God. I can only imagine the joy in the heart of the paralytic man. But the miracle wasn't just for him. For the people who witnessed it, the man's healing was an opportunity to believe in Jesus.

Does your faith increase when you witness a miracle? If you're anything like me, the answer is a big fat yes! When we hear miracle stories or witness evidence of a miracle, our faith does indeed increase. But Jesus referred to those who seek only miraculous signs as "an evil and adulterous generation" (Matt. 12:39, MEV). We are to seek the Savior, not the signs and wonders He performs.

I think it's telling that the scripture says Jesus saw their faith—faith to be healed and faith to be saved.

FASTING FOR PATIENCE

Now there was one, Anna, a prophetess, the daughter of Phanuel, of the tribe of Asher. She was of a great age and had lived with a husband seven years from her virginity; and this woman was a widow of about eighty-four years, who did not depart from the temple, but served God with fastings and prayers night and day. And coming in that instant she gave thanks to the Lord, and spoke of Him to all those who looked for redemption in Jerusalem.

—LUKE 2:36–38

FASTING LESSON

How long do you have to pray and believe before you see the hand of God move? I'm not sure, but one of my favorite stories in the Bible is the story of Anna. She was in her eighties and yet had not given up on seeing the answer to her prayer.

She stood day and night in the temple courtyard in prayer and fasting, believing that one day her eyes would see Jesus. More than anything, she wanted to see the promised Messiah. More than she wanted relief from the pain that comes with age or the loneliness of being a widow, she wanted to see Jesus.

I have often wondered what I will be known and remembered for. What will my story be? When I am eighty-plus years old, will I still be pursuing the things of God? I hope so.

How about you? Do you have the faith of Anna? Do you desire to see Jesus with all that is in you?

Anna's fast fueled her faith. In God's perfect timing, as Anna stood in the temple courtyard, Mary and Joseph walked into the temple with the child Jesus to do for Him according to the custom of the Law. Her prayer was answered. Her fast was seen. Her faith was honored.

Are you willing to wait for your miracle?

REFLECTION TIME

If you were lying on a stretcher and your friends brought you to Jesus, do you think it would be odd to hear Him say, "Your sins are forgiven"? I think the moment the paralytic looked into Jesus' eyes, he knew he had met the Savior. When we are face to face with our Lord, things get very real very quick. Jesus has the power to both forgive sin and heal bodies. Do you need physical healing today? Do you need forgiveness of sin? Talk to Jesus now. He is here for you just as He was for the paralytic.

_____

_____

_____

Do you seek signs and wonders or the heart of the Father? Miracles are supernatural and divine, but we must never desire a miracle so badly that we focus on it more than the glory of God. Do you think about receiving your miracle more often than pleasing the Father?

_____

_____

_____

What do you think you will be doing at eighty years of age? Will you be resting, reflecting, or waiting for Jesus to come through with your request? Write a note to your eighty-year-old self, encouraging you to stay strong and expectant in faith. As you write, describe what you want to be doing in your old age for the kingdom.

_____

_____

_____

_____

_____

_____

_____

_____

_____

_____

_____

_____

CLOSING PRAYER

Dear Lord, I commit myself to seeking Your will for my life. I ask that You help me stay consistent and faithful in my daily walk with You. Teach me to keep my eyes faithfully on You and Your kingdom. In Jesus' name, amen.

JOURNAL ENTRY

_____

_____

_____

_____

_____

_____

_____

_____

_____

_____

day
17

WIND
and
WAVES

WE KNOW INTELLECTUALLY that God is supernatural—that He exists above the natural, physical world. But it still shocks the system to read that Jesus overruled the laws of nature and calmed a raging storm with His words and even walked on water, as we'll see in today's stories. God is not limited by the rules of the physical world. He is almighty and all-powerful. The things that look impossible to us are no sweat for the God we serve.

SCRIPTURE READINGS

Now when He got into a boat, His disciples followed Him. And suddenly a great tempest arose on the sea, so that the boat was covered with the waves. But He was asleep. Then His disciples came to Him and awoke Him, saying, "Lord, save us! We are perishing!"

But He said to them, "Why are you fearful, O you of little faith?" Then He arose and rebuked the winds and the sea, and there was a great calm. So the men marveled, saying, "Who can this be, that even the winds and the sea obey Him?"

—MATTHEW 8:23–27

Immediately Jesus made His disciples get into the boat and go before Him to the other side, while He sent the multitudes away. And when He had sent the multitudes away, He went up on the mountain by Himself to pray. Now when evening came, He was alone there. But the boat was now in the middle of the sea, tossed by the waves, for the wind was contrary.

Now in the fourth watch of the night Jesus went to them, walking on the sea. And when the disciples saw Him walking on the sea, they were troubled, saying, "It is a ghost!" And they cried out for fear. But immediately

Jesus spoke to them, saying, "Be of good cheer! It is I; do not be afraid." And Peter answered Him and said, "Lord, if it is You, command me to come to You on the water."

So He said, "Come." And when Peter had come down out of the boat, he walked on the water to go to Jesus. But when he saw that the wind was boisterous, he was afraid; and beginning to sink he cried out, saying, "Lord, save me!" And immediately Jesus stretched out His hand and caught him, and said to him, "O you of little faith, why did you doubt?" And when they got into the boat, the wind ceased.

Then those who were in the boat came and worshiped Him, saying, "Truly You are the Son of God."

—MATTHEW 14:22–33

> "Now when He got into a boat,
> His disciples followed Him.
>
> —MATTHEW 8:23"

MIRACLE
PASSAGE

JESUS DEFIES NATURE

I live in Southern California, and one of my favorite summer activities is to boat across the Pacific to Catalina Island. A few years back, our friends invited us to take the journey across the water and stay with them overnight on their yacht. It sounded luxurious, fascinating, and fun—that is, until a storm hit. While we were docked at a cove near the island, the wind and waves kicked up. To say I did not sleep a wink that night is an understatement. I was scared to death.

I can relate to these disciples. Even if you're a good swimmer, the feel of restless waves crashing beneath you is frightening. But Jesus commands the wind and the waves, as we saw in both of our Scripture passages today. He is in control of the seas.

I'm sure you have had times of testing in your life—times of restless seas. In those moments God is calling you to a deeper faith.

Did you notice that Matthew 8:24 says Jesus was asleep? Jesus can rest in the midst of a storm, and we can rest in Him when we're being tossed by the winds and waves of life. Jesus only awoke to meet the needs of those with Him, not necessarily to calm the storm. He was not affected by the storm; He was affected by the cry of His disciples.

In Matthew 14, after He kept Peter from drowning, Jesus said, "O you of little faith, why did you doubt?" (v. 31). Jesus is always looking for ways to increase our faith. In today's miracle stories, Jesus was not only teaching Peter and the other disciples to trust Him in the storm; He was teaching them to trust

Him over the storm. Not only did the wind and waves calm at Jesus' command, but He defied the laws of nature by walking on the water. You could say He was surfing without a board!

Whether you are in a situation filled with uncertainty or Jesus is calling you to take a step of faith and "walk on water," you can be assured that Jesus is always in control. The storms in your life still must obey Him.

> He was not affected by the storm; He was affected by the cry of His disciples.

FASTING FOR CLARITY AND STRENGTH

FASTING PASSAGE

When they had preached the gospel to that city and had made many disciples, they returned to Lystra and to Iconium and to Antioch, strengthening the minds of the disciples and exhorting them to continue in the faith, to go through many afflictions and thus enter the kingdom of God. When they had appointed elders for them in every church, with prayer and fasting, they commended them to the Lord in whom they believed.

—ACTS 14:21–23, MEV

FASTING LESSON

In the Book of Acts, Jesus had ascended to heaven, the gospel was spreading, and the Holy Spirit was moving. Persecution had come on the church, and the enemy was attacking those who followed Jesus. The apostles knew they needed godly leadership to sustain this new movement. And with prayer and fasting, they began to appoint leaders and elders to guide the burgeoning churches.

Fasting can bring clarity and divine revelation. When you are in the midst of a decision, fasting is a tool you can use to hear from the heart of God.

Fasting can also give us strength. I don't believe we have seen the type of persecution and "afflictions" the believers in the New Testament experienced. I do, however, believe that since the pandemic in 2020, the enemy has been unleashed to bring fear and harassment on the church. There are those like my good friend Sean Feucht who have experienced great ridicule and persecution for his faith.

His movement, Let Us Worship, has endured the enemy's plot to silence the church. He and many other believers stood strong through the pandemic, refusing to give up their voices and their rights, and we must continue to do so. This is not the time for the church to be silent. This is the time for the church to speak up and speak out, to be set free and stand strong. Do not be fearful or buy in to the schemes of the enemy. Be faithful in the calling of Christ. Fasting can strengthen your resolve to stand firm in the power of the Holy Spirit.

God may be prompting you to take action in a certain area of your life. Today's fasting lesson teaches us to ask for clarity and divine direction every day. This is a good time to build your faith and fortitude for your future. As 2 Timothy 4:2 tells us, "Preach the word! Be ready in season and out of season. Convince, rebuke, exhort, with all longsuffering and teaching."

I believe fasting gives us the heart of our Father. God is moving in our world today. Press in to the supernatural realm of God and see your miracle become reality.

REFLECTION TIME

Have you ever had a traumatic experience while boating, swimming, or enjoying some other activity in the water? If so, you can relate to the disciples. How did you feel? Were you scared, unsure, nervous? The good news is God can calm your storm. He can quiet your seas. Whatever is causing you to feel fearful or uncertain today, God's got it. What do you need God to do in your life that would bring a sense of peace and calm?

_____

_____

_____

_____

I don't like difficulty. Yet the Bible tells us in John 16:33 that in the world we will have tribulation. Why do you think that is? Could it be so we will seek God for clarity and wisdom? I will say that the hardest times in my life have proven to be the most valuable. Describe a time in your life when God used a hardship to prove His grace or instruct you.

_____

_____

_____

_____

The pandemic proved to be a time of great reflection. The enemy brought fear and uncertainty on every front. This twenty-one-day fast is a great time to ask God for wisdom and direction for your future. Go deep with God and ask Him how you can stand strong in your faith. I believe it is time for Christians to raise their voices. By sharing your testimony, you can make a difference in someone's life for eternity. What action steps are you willing to take to boldly proclaim your faith?

CLOSING PRAYER

Dear Lord, I want to be bold and courageous. Show me how to use my life for Your kingdom. Give me clarity and wisdom for the days ahead. I trust that You are working things together for my good. In Jesus' name, amen.

JOURNAL ENTRY

_____

_____

_____

_____

_____

_____

_____

_____

_____

_____

day
18

RAISING the DEAD

WE'VE ALREADY SEEN that nothing is too hard for God. Today's story is a reminder that even death doesn't stand a chance in His presence.

SCRIPTURE READING

While He spoke these things to them, behold, a ruler came and worshiped Him, saying, "My daughter has just died, but come and lay Your hand on her and she will live." So Jesus arose and followed him, and so did His disciples.

And suddenly, a woman who had a flow of blood for twelve years came from behind and touched the hem of His garment. For she said to herself, "If only I may touch His garment, I shall be made well." But Jesus turned around, and when He saw her He said, "Be of good cheer, daughter; your faith has made you well." And the woman was made well from that hour.

When Jesus came into the ruler's house, and saw the flute players and the noisy crowd wailing, He said to them, "Make room, for the girl is not dead, but sleeping." And they ridiculed Him. But when the crowd was put outside, He went in and took her by the hand, and the girl arose. And the report of this went out into all that land.

—MATTHEW 9:18-26

The enemy will always try to challenge the power of God, and it is often in the moment just before the miracle that the enemy will show out the most!

He said to them, "Make room, for the girl is not dead, but sleeping." And they ridiculed Him. But when the crowd was put outside, He went in and took her by the hand, and the girl arose. And the report of this went out into all that land.

—MATTHEW 9:24–26

MIRACLE PASSAGE

RESURRECTING HOPE

This is when your miracle gets real: you think it's too late, you think it's over, you think God has given up, then Jesus walks into the room and says, "Make room for the miracle!"

In these stories, we have two situations that would seem to be "too late" for God to move from a human point of view. For the unnamed woman with the issue of blood, twelve years was a long time to deal with both the physical discomfort of chronic bleeding and the social stigma that went with her condition. As if being unwell wasn't bad enough, this situation meant she was perpetually viewed as unclean. If there is anything worse than dealing with a terrible illness, it is surely dealing with that sickness while feeling the judgment of your community. Twelve years of physical and mental anguish would be long enough for anyone to give up hope.

Yet this woman, who had every natural reason to believe it was "too late," recognized her answer when she saw Jesus. How many times had she reached for some kind of solution, some kind of answer, only to be disappointed? And yet she reached out for Jesus. She reached out to Him because some part of her recognized that He had the power to change her situation. This is how it is with the things of God: it is too late—until it isn't. It is beyond all hope—until suddenly hope comes walking by. It is utterly impossible—until God does it.

We can imagine all the reasons the woman may have told herself it was too late for a touch from God, but in the second story the ruler's daughter

MIRACLE STORY

was clearly dead. Everyone was trying to tell Jesus it was too late. Knowing how the story ends, it's easy for us to judge the crowd for being so willing to give up on believing the girl could be saved. But the irony is that we all do it. When we are tired or exhausted, when the situation has gone on too long, when we have sought answers and nothing has changed—we too have given up hope. We have also told Jesus it's too late. But it's *never* too late. In the right moment, Jesus will say to you, "Make some room; I'm getting ready to work." It's hard to know how long to wait, how long to keep asking or even expecting. As we have seen throughout these stories, miracles do not come on command—they come by faith.

Jesus taught His disciples to speak it out, call it out, and believe for it. Jesus waits for the perfect moment to show His glory, His sufficiency, His heart. His timing is not our timing. But when we think we are out of time, we are just in time for a miracle.

Today I want you to look at your need differently. Sometimes we need to become desperate, to rule out all other options: the option of doubt, the option of just accepting life the way it is, the option of being disappointed with God. Sometimes every option has to be exhausted—except to cry out for God.

Sometimes our desperate cry is exactly what God is looking for.

God made us in His image; therefore we have great ability and often too much self-confidence. Sometimes we can get in the way of our miracle because we lose sight of our need.

I don't know where you are right now. Maybe you think it's too late. Maybe it's not just the voice inside you but the voices around you that have told you it's been too long. Or maybe you are desperate and still have faith enough to reach for God as your only answer. If that is you, please don't stop expecting a miracle.

Whether you are like the father desperate to save his daughter or the woman with the issue of blood, only Jesus can meet your need and completely heal you of your heartache. Your moment may not have come yet, but when Jesus comes by, it only takes a moment for everything to change.

FASTING FOR HEALING

FASTING PASSAGE

And when He came to the disciples, He saw a great multitude around them, and scribes disputing with them. Immediately, when they saw Him, all the people were greatly amazed, and running to Him, greeted Him. And He asked the scribes, "What are you discussing with them?"

Then one of the crowd answered and said, "Teacher, I brought You my son, who has a mute spirit. And wherever it seizes him, it throws him down; he foams at the mouth, gnashes his teeth, and becomes rigid. So I spoke to Your disciples, that they should cast it out, but they could not."

He answered him and said, "O faithless generation, how long shall I be with you? How long shall I bear with you? Bring him to Me." Then they brought him to Him. And when he saw Him, immediately the spirit convulsed him, and he fell on the ground and wallowed, foaming at the mouth. So He asked his father, "How long has this been happening to him?"

And he said, "From childhood. And often he has thrown him both into the fire and into the water to destroy him. But if You can do anything, have compassion on us and help us." Jesus said to him, "If you can believe, all things are possible to him who believes." Immediately the father of the child cried out and said with tears, "Lord, I believe; help my unbelief!"

When Jesus saw that the people came running together, He rebuked the unclean spirit, saying to it, "Deaf and dumb spirit, I command you, come out of him and enter him no more!" Then the spirit cried out, convulsed him greatly, and came out of him. And he became as one dead, so that many said, "He is dead." But Jesus took him by the hand and lifted him up, and he arose. And when He had come into the house, His disciples asked Him privately, "Why could we not cast it out?" So He said to them, "This kind can come out by nothing but prayer and fasting."

—MARK 9:14–29

FASTING LESSON

Several times already we have considered this often-overlooked line in which Jesus tells His disciples that "this kind can come out by nothing but prayer and fasting." Now let's go deeper into the backstory: The disciples and the scribes were in a dispute over the miracles of Jesus. The father and the boy found themselves caught in the middle of the debate. But when the demonic spirit encountered Jesus, he manifested through the boy. The enemy will always try to challenge the power of God, and it is often in the moment just before the miracle that the enemy will show out the most! In desperation, the father cried out, "Jesus, please, if You can do anything, help us!" This was the moment.

"If you believe, all things are possible," Jesus replied to the father. "Lord, I believe," the man said. "Help my unbelief."

Let's take a moment to examine that response. The father had gone to great pains to get his son to Jesus. He was undeterred by the crowds. The very fact that he had made it to such a moment and was now crying out to Jesus demonstrated that he believed Jesus could help his son. Yet in his heart he knew there had been times of doubting.

I love this passage because it shows the Bible is honest and gives us the resources to be honest with ourselves. There will be times when our faith is strong, when we do not waver in our beliefs. But then there will be times when we doubt, times when we give up—times when hopelessness, fear, and discouragement overwhelm us.

Those are the times when we cry out to God, "Help my unbelief!" Jesus heard his cry. He healed his son. The disciples and scribes and followers of Jesus all witnessed a miracle—a miracle of a young boy being set free from a demonic spirit. But they also witnessed a lesson in faith: when you have moments of doubt, be honest with God. Ask Him to increase your faith and perform a miracle.

It was in this context that Jesus spoke these words: "This kind can come out by nothing but prayer and fasting" (v. 29). Some things in our lives take more than prayer. They take fasting with faith. Fasting allows us to go deeper into our need, deeper into our dependence on God. Fasting removes all the clutter and noise that keep us from looking to God in faith.

If you are struggling today for a breakthrough, exercise your faith as you fast. Use this time to dig deep into the heart and ways of God. Your miracle *is* on its way. God is working.

REFLECTION TIME

Everywhere Jesus turned, there was someone who needed help. Yet when the father told Jesus about his daughter's death, Jesus rose immediately. While Jesus was on His way, a woman hemorrhaging reached out for healing. Jesus stopped and heard her cry. Jesus is our help in times of trouble. Where do you need Jesus to heal you today?

_____

_____

_____

_____

It seems that in Mark 9 the disciples were caught in a discussion about the miracles of Jesus. There will always be debates about whether God can truly heal and perform miracles. But remember what Jesus said: "All things are possible to him who believes" (v. 23, MEV). Have you had times of doubting that God will answer your prayer? If so, let me ask you: Do you believe all things are possible? Take a few moments now and speak life over your request. Renew your faith and declare, "With God all things are possible." Write those declarations of faith.

_____

_____

_____

_____

When the disciples asked Jesus why they could not cast out the demon, He responded, "This kind can come out by nothing but prayer and fasting" (Mark 9:29). I'm not sure what He was referring to when He said "this kind," but I know some things are demonic and need supernatural power and authority to make them flee. Mark 9:29 reminds us that fasting is key to seeing our breakthrough. As you fast, you are perhaps coming into a more direct confrontation with "this kind" of oppression and resistance. Perhaps you feel yourself in more direct conflict with the enemy. As you take an inventory of your fast so far, are you able to see more clearly what obstacles need to be removed (or the obstacles God is already removing)? The unclean spirit in the boy began convulsing and acting out just before Jesus cast the spirit out and healed him. Is anything in your life starting to quiver as you press in closer to Jesus? Are some things suddenly looking worse instead of better? Or are you seeing signs that your miracle is on its way?

_____

_____

_____

_____

CLOSING PRAYER

Dear Lord, I want to see breakthrough and power. You know how much I need healing and hope. God, I ask in faith that You work a miracle in my life. Show me Your glory. I will continue to trust and obey You along the journey. You alone are worthy of praise and honor. In Jesus' name, amen.

JOURNAL ENTRY

_____

_____

_____

_____

_____

_____

_____

_____

_____

_____

_____

_____

_____

_____

_____

day
19

FEEDING
the
MULTITUDES

Today's miracle story about Jesus feeding the five thousand is a clear reminder that we serve a God who is more than enough. Jesus plus nothing is enough to meet all our needs.

SCRIPTURE READING

When Jesus heard this, He departed from there by boat for a deserted place. But when the people heard it, they followed Him on foot from the cities. Jesus went ashore and saw a great assembly. And He was moved with compassion toward them, and He healed their sick.

When it was evening, His disciples came to Him, saying, "This is a lonely place and the day is now over. Send the crowds away to go into the villages and buy themselves food."

But Jesus said to them, "They do not need to depart. You give them something to eat."

They said to Him, "We have only five loaves here and two fish."

He said, "Bring them here to Me." Then He commanded the crowds to sit down on the grass. He took the five loaves and the two fish, and looking up to heaven, He blessed and broke and gave the loaves to His disciples; and the disciples gave them to the crowds. They all ate and were filled. And they took up twelve baskets full of the fragments that remained. Those who had eaten were about five thousand men, besides women and children.

—MATTHEW 14:13–21, MEV

I believe miracles are all around us. The problem is we don't always recognize them.

"

Then He commanded the crowds to sit down on the grass. He took the five loaves and the two fish, and looking up to heaven, He blessed and broke and gave the loaves to His disciples; and the disciples gave them to the crowds. They all ate and were filled. And they took up twelve baskets full of the fragments that remained.

—MATTHEW 14:19–20, MEV

"

MIRACLE PASSAGE

A MIRACULOUS MEAL

Even Jesus had those moments when He just needed to get away and pray. He had times when He would steal away to be alone, reflect, and rest. But this was not to be one of those times. Just as Jesus finally found the solitude and tranquility of a deserted place, He was pulled away from His seclusion by the crowds.

The masses had been following His miracles, His acts of kindness, and His message of salvation. When they heard where Jesus was, they followed Him there. True to His nature, Jesus healed the sick and destitute, the blind and depressed. It had already been a long day for Jesus, but His heart ached with compassion for the crowd.

As the sun began to set, the disciples became concerned with how they would feed the masses. "Jesus, what will we do to feed the multitude?" They had already seen the miracles of Jesus, but like some of us who have also seen the miracles of Jesus, we still have moments when we are overwhelmed by the magnitude of the needs in front of us. As the disciples were caught up in the anxiety of the moment, they forgot that Jesus was a mighty Miracle Worker, the divine Son of God. They did not ask in faith; they asked in flesh. They asked with their understanding, not with their hearts.

Jesus did what He always does; He made something out of nothing. "Go and gather all the fish and loaves that you can find and bring them back to Me," He said. This would be a miracle for both the disciples and the people. Did you notice in the story that Jesus said to the disciples, "You give them something to eat"? Jesus was getting ready to perform a miracle through the hands of the disciples. He blessed the loaves and fish and then handed them to the disciples to disperse. As we know, everyone was fed. They even had leftovers—twelve baskets full, possibly one for each disciple.

Have you ever had a dinner party and more people showed up than planned? You set the food out buffet style and just pray it will be enough. I'm sure that's how the disciples felt as they passed out the loaves and fish, holding their breath and praying there would be enough to go around.

That's the story of the loaves and fish. God multiplied the miracle for both the disciples and the people.

I believe miracles are all around us. The problem is we don't always recognize them. We too get caught up in the anxiety of the moment. We too get swallowed up by the need staring us down. We may even have believed God for a miracle before, but in the moment it feels impossible to see how on earth the need could ever be met. Yet we serve a miracle-working God who is sustaining, protecting, and providing for His people every step of the way. He has provided for us before, and He's going to provide for us again. What daunting need is overwhelming you in this moment? Have you been afraid there will not be enough? Do you need your loaves and fish multiplied?

If you are running dry on resources, God may ask you what is already in your hand. We get so fixated on what we don't have that we lose sight of what God has already given us. Whatever God has placed in your hand, give it back to the Miracle Worker and watch your faith expand.

FASTING FOR HUMILITY

Cry aloud, spare not; lift up your voice like a trumpet; tell My people their transgression, and the house of Jacob their sins. Yet they seek Me daily, and delight to know My ways, as a nation that did righteousness, and did not forsake the ordinance of their God. They ask of Me the ordinances of justice; they take delight in approaching God. "Why have we fasted," they say, "and You have not seen? Why have we afflicted our souls, and You take no notice?"

In fact, in the day of your fast you find pleasure, and exploit all your laborers. Indeed you fast for strife and debate, and to strike with the fist of wickedness. You will not fast as you do this day, to make your voice heard on high. Is it a fast that I have chosen, a day for a man to afflict his soul? Is it to bow down his head like a bulrush, and to spread out sackcloth and ashes? Would you call this a fast, and an acceptable day to the Lord? Is this not the fast that I have chosen: to loose the bonds of wickedness, to undo the heavy burdens, to let the oppressed go free, and that you break every yoke? Is it not to share your bread with the hungry, and that you bring to your house the poor who are cast out; when you see the naked, that you cover him, and not hide yourself from your own flesh?

Then your light shall break forth like the morning, your healing shall spring forth

282

speedily, and your righteousness shall go before you; the glory of the Lord shall be your rear guard. Then you shall call, and the Lord will answer; you shall cry, and He will say, "Here I am." If you take away the yoke from your midst, the pointing of the finger, and speaking wickedness, if you extend your soul to the hungry and satisfy the afflicted soul, then your light shall dawn in the darkness, and your darkness shall be as the noonday. The Lord will guide you continually, and satisfy your soul in drought, and strengthen your bones; you shall be like a watered garden, and like a spring of water, whose waters do not fail. Those from among you shall build the old waste places; you shall raise up the foundations of many generations; and you shall be called the Repairer of the Breach, the Restorer of Streets to Dwell In.

—Isaiah 58:1–12

FASTING LESSON

Talk about a convicting passage! Each time I read these verses, I must reflect upon my own heart. "Cry out loud," the prophet says. "Be honest and truthful with My people. They say they delight in My goodness, but their righteousness is far from it. They are fasting as a ritual, yet their wickedness is clearly seen. Unkind acts, pride, and self-sufficiency have become the norm. This is not the fast I desire," God says.

Although the children of Israel were fasting, they were ignoring the clear instructions from God to meet the needs of the less fortunate among them and to treat them with dignity and worth. Fasting should result in humility and self-denial, not in pride and self-indulgence. In the words of Psalm 35:13, "I humbled my soul with fasting" (MEV).

The evidence of a godly fast is humility. This is the fast the Lord has chosen. We've mentioned several times throughout the twenty-one-day journey that God does honor our fast. He tells us to fast. But we are to fast with His agenda at heart, not our own. In Isaiah's day, the people were more interested in looking self-righteous than in doing what pleased God.

True fasting leads to humility and a universal testimony to humanity.

Today is a good day to examine your heart. Are you staying faithful to your commitment? Are you still expecting a miracle? Or has your fast become a ritual or possibly even an idol? Those are strong words, I know. But we can make anything an idol. Anything we put before God is an idol—even our spiritual acts of service.

One final observation from this passage. Notice the Lord said through the prophet, "They seek Me daily, and delight to know My ways, as a nation that did righteousness, and did not forsake the ordinance of their God" (Isa. 58:2).

This truth is for us today. We have division and jealousy in our churches. Pride, anger, and gossip have entered the doors of many congregations. As a nation, we are calling on God for help, direction, and guidance, but we don't see that we have moved away from the blessing and power of God. We, like the nation of Israel, must turn, repent, and bow our heads to the One and only God. We need a national fast and corporate revival to heal our hearts and homes. Are you prepared to ask God for a national movement of His Spirit? Are you ready to be broken and humble enough to care for the needs of others before yourself? Are you ready to see the captives set free? This is the type of fast the Lord requires.

REFLECTION TIME

Did you notice in today's miracle story that the disciples told Jesus to send the people into town so they could get something to eat? Jesus had been working miracles all day, yet they did not consider that He could provide dinner. God created you body, soul, and spirit. He cares about you physically and spiritually. All dimensions are important. You are created in His image. Take a full inventory of every area of your life today. Don't assume any need that matters to you does not matter to God. In what areas do you need a miracle?

_____

_____

_____

_____

Five loaves and two fish fed five thousand men; that doesn't include the women and children. Now that's a miracle! To top it off, they had leftovers. God is the God of more than enough. In what areas do you need God's abundance—finances, friendship, family, favor? God can supply everything you need, but you must ask in faith. In your own words, ask Jesus to feed your soul right now.

_____

_____

_____

_____

Today we are fasting for humility. Our scripture reminds us that God wants a pure heart and right motive when we fast. Over these twenty-one days, we have been asking God for our faith to become our reality. God does work miracles. He does heal, redeem, and set free. But we must approach Him with humility and honor. From a place of humility, dependence, and trust, revisit the question, What do you want to see God do in your life?

_____

_____

_____

CLOSING PRAYER

Dear Lord, I know You care about me completely—body, soul, and spirit. I ask that every dimension of my life be wholly surrendered to You. Show me where I need to release any pride or self-sufficiency. I humbly ask to be filled with Your Spirit today. Lead, guide, and direct my steps. In Jesus' name, amen.

JOURNAL ENTRY

_____

_____

_____

day 20

THE BOOK OF Acts is filled with incredible demonstrations of the Holy Spirit's power, and today's miracle story is no exception. An angel literally opened prison doors and freed the apostles. Let that sink in. Whatever prison you find yourself in is no match for God.

SCRIPTURE READING

And through the hands of the apostles many signs and wonders were done among the people. And they were all with one accord in Solomon's Porch. Yet none of the rest dared join them, but the people esteemed them highly. And believers were increasingly added to the Lord, multitudes of both men and women, so that they brought the sick out into the streets and laid them on beds and couches, that at least the shadow of Peter passing by might fall on some of them. Also a multitude gathered from the surrounding cities to Jerusalem, bringing sick people and those who were tormented by unclean spirits, and they were all healed.

Then the high priest rose up, and all those who were with him (which is the sect of the Sadducees), and they were filled with indignation, and laid their hands on the apostles and put them in the common prison. But at night an angel of the Lord opened the prison doors and brought them out, and said, "Go, stand in the temple and speak to the people all the words of this life." And when they heard that, they entered the temple early in the morning and taught. But the high priest and those with him came and called the council together, with all the elders of the children of Israel, and sent to the prison to have them brought.

—ACTS 5:12-21

There are angels around us even now, poised to respond to God's command to release us from our prison cells.

> "But at night an angel of the Lord opened the prison doors and brought them out, and said, "Go, stand in the temple and speak to the people all the words of this life."
>
> —Acts 5:19-20

MIRACLE PASSAGE

PRISON DOORS OPEN

Now *this* is a miracle story. People were literally healed by the shadow of the apostle Peter. What are we to make of this?

After Jesus was resurrected, He said He must go away but that He would send the Holy Spirit, the Comforter. He said that He would be in us and with us. Acts, then, is a book full of accounts of what happened when the Spirit was poured out on those early disciples. Divine power and supernatural miracles were happening through the apostles.

But as it is with any of us, the presence of the Holy Spirit in our lives doesn't mean the road will be without resistance. The fact that powerful signs and wonders are at work also doesn't mean everyone will be drawn to follow Jesus.

Even as all these extraordinary miracles were happening, some were afraid to join them. The Scripture says they "esteemed them highly" (Acts 5:13), meaning they were impressed with their power and faith yet weren't willing to join them. They were observers, not participants. But there were others who eagerly joined them, both men and women.

The Holy Spirit is on the move in our time too. The question is, Will you choose to be an observer or a participant in what God is doing? Do you want to see miracles? Do you want God to use you as an instrument of healing to those around you? You must answer those questions.

My next question is, Are you filled with the Holy Spirit of God? Do you know Jesus as your Lord and

Savior? And if you know Him, are you allowing the Holy Spirit to flow freely through your life—not obstructing His work with sin, doubt, or fear?

Supernaturally, God released the men from prison because He had an assignment for them to do. He had a role for them to play. He had a testimony for them to speak.

We all have an assignment, and that is to walk in the fullness of the Holy Spirit. I do believe this was a unique time in history. Miracles were flowing through the power of the Holy Spirit. I believe the purpose of the miracles was to confirm the message Jesus and the apostles proclaimed. But this does not minimize miracles today. I don't believe in magic handkerchiefs or religious shenanigans. I *do* believe in a good and faithful and honest God who still works miracles today.

Just as in New Testament times, there will be those who try to squelch miracles, to subdue and suppress them. But as it was for the apostles in this passage, and as it was for Paul and Silas, who would again be imprisoned a few chapters later, the work of the Holy Spirit will not be constricted or confined to small spaces.

The Sadducees tried to stop the miracle-working power of God by placing the apostles in jail. They thought prison would contain their power, but the power within them was not of their own making. It was the power of a living and active God. There are angels around us even now, poised to respond to God's command to release us from our prison cells. The question is, Are you ready to walk out of your prison? Are you ready to see miracles?

FASTING FOR FREEDOM

FASTING PASSAGE

As they worshipped the LORD and fasted, the Holy Spirit said, "Set apart for Me Barnabas and Saul for the work to which I have called them." Then after fasting and praying, they laid their hands on them and sent them off.

—ACTS 13:2–3, MEV

FASTING LESSON

I love the way this passage starts: as they worshipped and fasted, the Holy Spirit spoke. Do you understand the power of worship? I've heard people say they really don't like all the worship time at their church. It's too long, too loud—it's just too much.

Yet worship is what honors and exalts our God. Revelation 4 describes the throne of God. The saints are bowing down, worshipping Jesus, the Lamb of God. You can't help but worship and lift high the One who has redeemed your life from hell—the One who gives you hope and power and purpose and destiny. Worshipping is an act of honor and praise, and when you couple that with fasting, it is explosive!

Once again, the context is prayer and fasting.

After they had clarity about the assignment, they commissioned Saul and Barnabas to go as ambassadors of the gospel. It was a sending out, a confirmation of their common spirit. This passage teaches me the importance of calling together like-minded counsel for accountability. Through prayer, worship, fasting, and common hearts, these men were sent out to change the world.

This might be a good exercise for you to include when you're asking for your miracle: invite a few people with a like faith and character to join you on your fast. Spend some time in prayer and worship with them. Jesus said, "Where two or three are gathered together in My name, I am there in the midst of them" (Matt. 18:20).

When you gather with someone else who shares your heart and intention, Jesus meets with you. Now is the time to join with a community of people who share your love for God. Now is the time to push through for your miracle.

> # You can't help but worship and lift high the One who has redeemed your life from hell.

REFLECTION TIME

What a move of God! Acts 5:14 says that "believers were increasingly added to the Lord, multitudes of both men and women." Why? Was it because of the signs and wonders being done? Was it because of the miracles being manifested? Well, yes, I'm sure it was. But the real power is not in the miracle but in the Miracle Worker: Jesus. Sometimes we want our miracle more than we want our Maker. Which do you find yourself seeking today—the miracle or the Miracle Worker? Jesus wants to give us peace beyond all comprehension, but we have to focus our attention exclusively on Him.

_____

_____

_____

_____

The enemy cannot stop the power of God. He may try to control and capture your emotions, but God will send His angels to comfort and console your spirit. Do you feel like you are in prison? Maybe you need to be set free today. Do you feel stuck, discouraged, or angry? Take some time to reflect on whatever small, confining, constricting spaces you may be in that have kept you from entering into the full freedom of God—and then ask God to set you free from the prisons of this world.

_____

_____

_____

_____

Do you like to sing? I'll bet when you are all alone in your
car and an oldie but goodie pops up on the radio, you
begin to sing. That's because singing makes us happy—it
is a scientific fact. We were created to sing, to worship, to
rejoice. I love our worship time at Influence Church. We are
blessed with some of the most creative songwriters and
musicians. But while I love how worship makes me feel, the
truth is that worship is not about me. Worship is all about
Jesus. Our fasting passage today tells us that when they
were worshipping and fasting, the Holy Spirit showed up.
Take some time today and just worship the Lord. What is
your favorite worship song, and why does it mean so much
to you?

_____

_____

_____

_____

_____

_____

CLOSING PRAYER

Dear Lord, today I choose to worship and praise You alone. You are my Shepherd, my Rock, my Redeemer. I ask that You set me free from the prisons of this world—from all the fear, anxiety, anger, and lies. Give me Your perspective and peace, and guide me on life's journey. In Jesus' name, amen.

JOURNAL ENTRY

day 21

RESURRECTION

THE GREATEST MIRACLE is that God loved us so much He sent His Son to die and save us from our sins. Then He rose from the dead, conquering death and hell. Today we see that miracle through the eyes of Mary Magdalene, one of the women who lived it.

SCRIPTURE READING

But Mary stood outside at the tomb weeping. As she wept, she stooped down and looked into the tomb, and she saw two angels in white sitting where the body of Jesus had lain, one at the head and one at the feet.

They said to her, "Woman, why are you weeping?"

She said to them, "Because they have taken away my Lord, and I do not know where they have put Him." When she had said this, she turned around and saw Jesus standing, but she did not know that it was Jesus.

Jesus said to her, "Woman, why are you weeping? Whom are you seeking?"

Supposing Him to be the gardener, she said to Him, "Sir, if You have carried Him away, tell me where You have put Him, and I will take Him away."

Jesus said to her, "Mary." She turned and said to Him, "Rabboni!" (which means Teacher). Jesus said to her, "Stop holding on to Me, for I have not yet ascended to My Father. But go to My brothers and tell them, 'I am ascending to My Father and your Father, to My God and your God.'"

Mary Magdalene came and told the disciples that she had seen the Lord and that He had said these things to her.

On the evening of that first day of the week, the doors being locked where the disciples were assembled, for fear of the Jews, Jesus came and stood in their midst, and said to them, "Peace be with you." When He had said this, He showed them His hands and His side. The disciples were then glad when they saw the Lord.

So Jesus said to them again, "Peace be with you. As My Father has sent Me, even so I send you." When He had said this, He breathed on them and said to them, "Receive the Holy Spirit."

—JOHN 20:11–22, MEV

From creation to the resurrection, God has been performing miracles. He will continue to do so until He takes us into eternity.

" Jesus said to her, "Mary." She turned and said to Him, "Rabboni!" (which means Teacher). Jesus said to her, "Stop holding on to Me, for I have not yet ascended to My Father. But go to My brothers and tell them, 'I am ascending to My Father and your Father, to My God and your God.'"... Jesus performed many other signs in the presence of His disciples, which are not written in this book. But these are written that you might believe that Jesus is the Christ, the Son of God, and that believing you may have life in His name.

—JOHN 20:16–17, 30–31, MEV "

MIRACLE PASSAGE

THE EMPTY TOMB

The curtain had gone up, and it was the final act—the resurrection of Jesus. This was not just any miracle; it was the miracle upon which the story of God and all of history hangs.

Jesus' body had been beaten and abused. He was three days' dead in a grave, and yet in prophetic fulfillment of Scripture, He appeared—alive—to Mary Magdalene and then the disciples. Why Mary first, you might ask?

Only God truly knows, but I believe it was because of her faith. She was the one who went to the tomb first, and she was the one waiting for the miracle. She was the one who did not waver at the cross. And she was the one who first witnessed the miracle of the resurrection and then went to retrieve the disciples.

I love the resurrection story because it is where my salvation was birthed. Through the blood and atonement of Jesus, I am forgiven.

Have you ever said, "This is just my cross to bear," perhaps referring to a difficulty, heartache, or something you just can't get through? Have you considered taking your cross to Jesus? I know Jesus speaks of taking up our cross daily and following Him (Luke 9:23). But I am convinced many of the crosses we bear are not crosses Jesus has called us to pick up at all. In fact, they may be burdens He wants to deliver us from.

The answer to your problem may not look exactly the way you thought it would, as resurrection often takes on a form we never expected. But God can resurrect your hope. He can resurrect your heart. He can resurrect your body.

Jesus didn't just experience resurrection; He is resurrection. Jesus Himself said in John 11:25, "I am the resurrection and the life. He who believes in Me, though he may die, yet shall he live" (MEV).

Jesus, the One who is resurrection Himself, knows exactly what you need on your journey! Let Him walk with you. Let Him guide you. Let Him instruct you.

From creation to the resurrection, God has been performing miracles. He will continue to do so until He takes us into eternity.

My prayer for you is that over these twenty-one days, you have grown in your faith to believe in miracles. You may want to make fasting part of your regular routine in the days ahead. Just remember, the act of fasting is for *you*, and it is a discipline for the purification of your heart.

FASTING FOR PEACE

FASTING PASSAGE

"Now, therefore," says the LORD, "turn to Me with all your heart, with fasting, with weeping, and with mourning." So rend your heart, and not your garments; return to the LORD your God, for He is gracious and merciful, slow to anger, and of great kindness; and He relents from doing harm. Who knows if He will turn and relent, and leave a blessing behind Him—a grain offering and a drink offering for the LORD your God?

Blow the trumpet in Zion, consecrate a fast, call a sacred assembly; gather the people, sanctify the congregation, assemble the elders, gather the children and nursing babes; let the bridegroom go out from his chamber, and the bride from her dressing room. Let the priests, who minister to the LORD, weep between the porch and the altar; let them say, "Spare Your people, O LORD, and do not give Your heritage to reproach, that the nations should rule over them. Why should they say among the peoples, 'Where is their God?'"

—JOEL 2:12–17

FASTING LESSON

Today is the last day of our fast—and what an appropriate passage to conclude with. As we have seen over and over again, the hearts of humanity are quick to turn toward evil, to go after foreign idols and frivolous desires. People often ask, Why does God seem so angry in the Old Testament? Isn't it obvious? He heals and repairs and restores and forgives and loves and redeems, only to have His people turn their backs on Him again and again.

What does it take for God to get your attention? Often the chastening of God is for our good, to bring us back into His arms.

I love this passage from Joel because it tells us God will relent. God will hold back any judgment or correction if we only heed His instructions.

This is where the friction comes. Why do we have to obey God? Why do we have to surrender and worship Him? Because we are His children, and He is our Redeemer. Our will is often out of alignment with God's will, but fasting is a tool God gives us to bring our will into alignment with His. Instead of wanting whatever we have always wanted, we begin to want what God wants. It is when our will is brought into alignment with God's good desires for us that we will experience the reality of Psalm 37:4: when you delight yourself in the Lord, "He will give you the desires of your heart" (MEV).

Joel 2 continues with God promising to send grain, new wine, and olive oil, enough to satisfy fully; He tells His children He will restore the years the locust has eaten (vv. 23–26). Why? Because through a corporate fast the people of God saw their hearts and turned back to truth. God was faithful to His promise and poured out His Spirit on all people. Through prophecy, dreams, and visions, God met His children. And all who called on the name of the Lord were saved (vv. 27–30).

Today's passage is one of enlightenment. If I could teach anything through this book, it would be to remind you to humble yourself before God. When you fast, fast for the glory of God. Yes, fast for miracles and breakthroughs, for healing and hope—but fast with a pure heart.

My prayer for you is that you continue your journey and go deep into the heart and loving arms of God our Father—that you see miracles happen and what you're believing for become a reality.

REFLECTION TIME

Mary was the first to see the resurrected Jesus. Maybe it was her faith or her hope in the fact that God said He would never leave or forsake her (Deut. 31:8). Either way, God met her in a glorious moment. Being in the right place at the right time always pays off. Where do you spend your time? Are they places where Jesus would show up? You must make space for Jesus to come and speak to you. Where do you like to meet Jesus (at church, in nature, while prayer walking or worshipping)? Make a commitment to meet with Jesus there this week.

_____

_____

_____

_____

Mary did not recognize Jesus at first. Maybe the shock of the empty tomb was consuming her mind. But when He called her by name, she turned and knew Him immediately. Do you know Jesus knows you by name? Actually, He knew you before you were even born. God has a plan and a destiny for you. Take a few moments now and just soak in the presence and power of the resurrected Jesus. Thank Him for His love, grace, and salvation. Where or how might the resurrected Jesus be showing up in your life now, perhaps in a form that is so different from what you expected you simply have not recognized Him?

_____

_____

_____

_____

Joel 2:12–17 is such a perfect passage to end our fast. It
speaks of the power of repentance to bring peace and
healing. The people had once again strayed from God,
much like what is happening in our world today. If we ever
needed God to forgive our land, it is now. It's as if we're
looking in a mirror—history does not change, nor does
humanity. The ebb and flow of life keeps us reaching for
more, yet we know in our souls that God alone can satisfy our deepest desires. As you conclude your fast today,
take some time to reflect on all God taught you over these
twenty-one days. What were your greatest highlights?

_____

_____

_____

_____

_____

_____

_____

_____

_____

CLOSING PRAYER

Dear Lord, thank You for meeting me on this journey. Your truth and insight have caused me to search my heart and grow in my faith. I ask that You stay close to me and continue to probe the recesses of my heart. I want my life to be a testimony of Your love and redemption. In Jesus' name, amen.

JOURNAL ENTRY

_____

_____

_____

_____

_____

_____

_____

_____

_____

_____

_____

MIRACLE TESTIMONIES

Miracles are all around us—every day someone receives a miracle. But sometimes the timing of our miracle is not what we would choose. I want to take a moment and share with you a few miracle testimonies of people I know personally. I want to encourage your faith and remind you that miracles really do still happen, and they can happen for and in you and the people you love. As you read these stories and rejoice in their beauty, take a moment to thank God that your own story is still unfolding— and your own miracle is still on the way!

It is hard to know exactly what to expect when starting a new church, but we hoped and prayed that Influence Church would be a place where God would do exactly what His Word promised. We lived every day with a sense of expectation. Little did we know that we would see countless miracles, the first of which took place within the first two months of the church's existence.

ARIEL

Ariel, a twenty-six-year-old mother of three, was diagnosed with a brain tumor the size of a grapefruit. I knew, as did all who gathered around Ariel to pray, that this was not how life should be. The Father was not using this sickness to punish her. Sickness is contrary to the way the kingdom is supposed to work, and it is our job to release all the promises of God on the earth. Only then will the world understand that God is good.

It was during this time that I began to truly

316

understand both the goodness of the Father and the power of hope. From here, I will let Ariel tell her own story:

I asked God, "Please make me a miracle. Lord, I have three babies and one with special needs; they need me." The next Sunday at Influence, I met with Pastor Phil, Tammy, and many other amazing people who prayed over me. I felt something supernatural happen that day. The next week I met with the neurosurgeon to discuss the results of my latest MRI. The doctor walked in and said very nonchalantly, "Well, the tumor is barely visible." He had no explanation why the tumor had shrunk to being "barely visible," but I do! God can do anything through faith. And He was not done.

Four years later, Tammy was interviewing little Belle Marie, an eight-year-old who had prayed for a family friend. Belle Marie's friend Precious had been suffering from lung cancer and was told that she had only a short time to live.

When Belle Marie heard that distressing news, she ran to her friend Precious, put her arms around her, and said, "You will live; you will not die, in Jesus' name." Two weeks later the doctors told Precious the cancer was gone. When Belle Marie's mother asked her if she had heard about Precious, she replied, "She's healed, right?"

SUSAN

Twenty-five-year-old Susan, another member who was with us during our church's first year, shared her story with me:

On September 26, 2012, my bladder stopped functioning. My urethra closed up completely, making it impossible to do one of the most natural voluntary bodily actions. After surgery number ten, I was ready to give up! It was then that members of the Influence prayer team prayed, asking God to rid me of all the physical and emotional pain from my past and present. God answered my prayers. He heard my cry!

The doctor confirmed my faith—he looked at me with confusion and a smile. He shook my hand and said, "I don't know how you did it, but you did. Let's go take the tube out. Congratulations!" I immediately covered my face and cried. Overwhelmed with happiness, I said out loud, "Thank You, Jesus!"

LUCY

Lucy was just three-and-a-half years old when she was diagnosed with malignant skin cancer on her scalp. Her parents recalled:

Our first response was to have Pastor Phil and Tammy and the Influence prayer team pray for her complete healing. On July 2, 2014, we received a call from the doctor saying all signs of the cancer were gone! This is yet another testimony that Jesus still heals people. If you have a need that only God can answer, I encourage you to connect with the prayer ministry of Influence Church.

These are just a few of the testimonies we've received over the years. God is still a Miracle Worker. Expect your breakthrough!

Hᴇʀᴇ's sᴏᴍᴇᴛʜɪɴɢ ᴛᴏ think about: What if God doesn't answer your prayer? What happens if you don't receive your miracle?

These questions pose a difficult response. Yes, there have been times in all our lives when we did not receive the miracle we asked for—hoped for, prayed for, and possibly even fasted for. We wonder, "Where are You, God? Can You hear me? Is it something I have done, or is my request something You just won't do?"

The truth is that we don't always get our miracle. Does that mean God is mad or, worse yet, indifferent and just doesn't care?

Maybe we try to make the situation super-spiritual and apply Romans 8:28: "all things work together for good to those who love God, to those who are called according to His purpose" (MEV). We just brush it off like it's something God is doing deep in our core for our good.

Or maybe we tell ourselves to wait, rest, believe, and have faith.

Something my husband once said really changed my life: simple answers to complex questions are bound to be wrong. I cannot give you a simple answer to complex questions. I do not know why God doesn't always give us the miracle we seek, especially when we're walking with Him, love Him, exercise our faith, and even fast and believe. God is God, and His ways truly are higher than ours. Maybe some of these experiences will never make sense to us now but will only make sense in light of the full healing God's sons and daughters will receive in eternity.

But it will not stop me from staying on the road

FINAL THOUGHTS

of expectation. I have been praying for a miracle for close to two years now that I still haven't received, and I am not giving up. I see evidence of my asking, evidence of my prayer, and now evidence of my faith. And I am still fasting for my miracle.

If you have not received your miracle, ask God why. I believe it's OK to ask Him questions. I would even go so far as to say God is in the midst of our questions. He is in the discovery of the answers. He is in the process. It's OK to have the hard conversations with God. He loves you and will always be there to hear your deepest desires. Never stop asking. Never stop believing. Never stop expecting your miracle.

If you have enjoyed the spiritual journey taken through *Fasting for Miracles*, let me encourage you to also read the first volume in this series, *Fasting With God*. You can find the book on Amazon or on my website, TammyHotsenpiller.com.

May God richly bless you in your coming and your going.

Tammy Hotsenpiller

INTRODUCTION

1. *Merriam-Webster*, s.v. "miracle," Merriam-Webster.com, accessed August 17, 2022, https://www.merriam-webster.com/dictionary/miracle.
2. Lee Strobel and Mark Mittelberg. "How Common Are Miracles?" thinke.org, December 13, 2021, https://thinke.org/blog/how-common-are-miracles-lee-strobel-amp-mark-mittelberg.
3. Bible Study Tools, s.v. "*dunamis*," accessed August 26, 2022, https://www.biblestudytools.com/lexicons/greek/nas/dunamis.html.
4. "How Many Miracles Are There in the Bible?," Spirit of Life Church, February 28, 2019, https://www.spiritoflifeag.com/how-many-miracles-are-there-in-the-bible/.
5. Richard J. Foster, *Celebration of Discipline* (San Francisco: Harper & Row, 1988), 47.

DAY 11

1. *Merriam-Webster*, s.v. "establish," Merriam-Webster.com, accessed August 27, 2022, https://www.merriam-webster.com/dictionary/establish.
2. Keith Bodner, *Elisha's Profile in the Book of Kings* (Oxford, UK: Oxford University Press, 2013), 10.
3. *Merriam-Webster*, s.v. "establish."

WEEK 3

1. "How Many Miracles Are There in the Bible?," Spirit of Life Church, February 28, 2019, https://www.spiritoflifeag.com/how-many-miracles-are-there-in-the-bible. John 20:30 and Acts 10:38–39 tell us that Jesus performed many other signs in the presence of His disciples that are not recorded in Scripture.

NOTES

ABOUT the AUTHOR

TAMMY HOTSENPILLER IS an author, speaker, life coach, and leader of a national women's movement. She is the president of Total Life Coach, a coaching company with an emphasis on life balance, purpose, and reinvention. She is also the founder and executive director of Women of Influence, an organization that seeks to educate and empower women in their spheres of influence (womenofinfluence.today).

Tammy and her husband, Phil, are the cofounders of Influence Church in Anaheim Hills, California. They live in Orange County, California, and have been blessed with three amazing children and seven grandchildren.

TAMMYHOTSENPILLER.COM